VALENTINO ROSSI

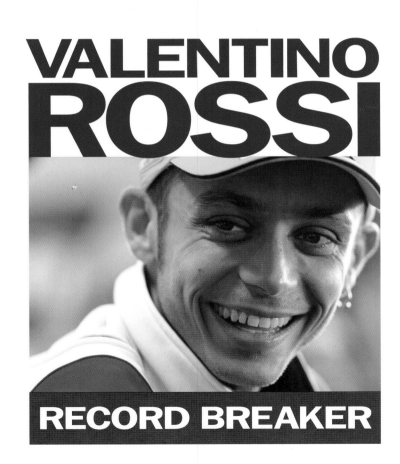

RECORD BREAKER

VALENTINO ROSSI

RECORD BREAKER

Text by
PETER McLAREN

Photography by
GOLD & GOOSE

CMG
PUBLISHING

Publisher
BRYN WILLIAMS

Text by
PETER McLAREN

Concept and Art Direction
STEVE SMALL

Design & Page Layout
ROSANNE MARRIOTT

Office Manager
WENDY SALISBURY

Crash Media Group Ltd
The Innovation Centre
Silverstone Circuit, Silverstone
Northants, NN12 8GX
Tel: +44 (0)870 3505044
Fax: +44 (0)870 3505088

info@crash.net
www.crashmediagroup.com

ISBN 978-1-905-334-51-3

Published in Italy by EditVallardi
via Roma 74–20060 Cassina de Pecchi
(Milan) – Italy

DISTRIBUTORS
Gardners Books
1 Whittle Drive, Eastbourne,
East Sussex BN23 6QH
Telephone: +44 (0)1323 521555
E-mail: sales@gardners.com

Printed in Italy by Poligrafica Antenore
via Perù 9/3–35127 Padova – Italy

Menoshire Ltd
Unit 13, 21 Wadsworth Road
Perivale, Middlesex UB6 7LQ
Telephone: +44 (0)20 8566 7344
Fax: +44 (0)20 8991 2439

North America
Motorbooks International
PO Box 1, 729 Prospect Avenue
Osceola, Wisconsin 54020, USA
Telephone: 1 715 294 3345
Fax: 1 715 294 4448

CONTENTS

Introduction	6
1996: The boy from Tuvullia makes his mark in the 125cc class.	12
1997: Valentino crushes the opposition with 11 victories from 15 races.	14
1998: 250cc debut, five wins and second only to Loris Capirossi.	24
1999: Dominant Champion. Rossi sweeps the 250cc class with 9 wins.	30
2000: Into the big league with Honda.	40
2001: Valentino's 500cc championship	44
2002: Enter MotoGP – but 'Valle' stays on top.	60
2003: A hat-trick of titles and farewell to Honda.	76
2004: Rossi takes Yamaha back to the top.	94
2005: Domination. Eleven wins, and a fifth successive championship.	110
2006: The man who fell to earth – Hayden snatches the title.	132
2007: Young gun Stoner and Ducati set the pace.	148
2008: 'The Doctor' bounces back. His greatest ever season?	160
2009: Valentino Rossi: Record-Breaker	182
Valentino Rossi's Grand Prix Career Record 1996-2009	185

Acknowledgements:

To Michael Scott for the use of text and quotations included in this publication that have previously appeared in MOTOCOURSE between 1996-2008.

INTRODUCTION

VALENTINO Rossi started the 2009 MotoGP World Championship back on top of the world and after his Spanish Grand Prix victory, stands just two wins short of a landmark 100 motorcycle Grand Prix victories across all three classes – 125cc, 250cc and 500cc/MotoGP. The statistics are awesome: One 125cc title, one 250cc title, one 500cc title and five MotoGP titles from 13 seasons of world championship racing with six different types of motorcycle – confirming Rossi as one of the most, if not the most talented rider the world has seen.

However, it is the human side of Rossi which has propelled him into a truly global superstar, famous beyond motorsport and supported by an army of die-hard fans at every race on the world championship calendar.

While many successful racers often display an air of arrogance while in pursuit of their goals, Rossi is the greatest entertainer in motorsport – his extravagant post race celebrations are legendary – and he has retained a fan-friendly persona in even the most stressful situations.

But don't be fooled, Rossi is also a ruthless competitor, mentally dismantling his opponents with seemingly light-hearted comments off the track and a master tactician on the track, never afraid to run across the dirt or bang handlebars in his seemingly insatiable desire for victory.

The son of grand prix racer Graziano Rossi, Valentino was born and raised in Tavullia, a small seaside town (near to the Misano Adriatico race track) on the north east coast of Italy, which has now become a virtual shrine to its most famous son.

"Tavullia is very small," said Rossi, who moved to London in 2000 to escape the pressures of fame in his home country. "It only has one street and is very quiet. It's a great place and is near the sea which is good in summer. A lot of my friends grew up there with me. I think I am lucky to have been born there."

Much of Valentino's laid back character seems to have been inherited from Graziano who – despite his son's fame – still sleeps in the back of a BMW estate car when he attends MotoGPs.

Graziano won three 250GPs on his way to third in the 1979 world championship, and then claimed two podiums to finish fifth overall in the 1980 500cc series.

"Graziano gave me a passion for motorcycles," said Rossi. "Maybe if Graziano had a different job or chose another sport I wouldn't have had this passion. Also, when I started racing he knew a lot of people in the sport and it was easier for me to get a ride at the start of my career."

Valentino and Graziano are only the third father and son in history to both win a motorcycle grand prix, although their riding 'styles' are somewhat different. "Graziano was quite crazy on a bike and even now, when he races a bike or a car, he always makes big mistakes!" smiled Rossi.

Inspired by his father's racing exploits, the young Valentino was soon showing an interest in motorcycles, although Graziano and mother, Stefania, felt a Go-Kart was a safer compromise.

Rossi continued along the four-wheeled path, winning his regional go-kart championship in 1990 and finishing fourth in the Italian Junior Go-Kart Championship the following season. But by then Rossi had also started racing minimotorcycles with almost instant success, and the costs of competition soon prompted the difficult decision to quit karts for bikes.

A regional minimoto champion in 1992, Rossi – who admits to being chased by the police as a youngster, due to his antics on a scooter – made the step up to a 'real' motorcycle the following year, when he finished third in the 125cc Italian Sports Production Championship on a Cagiva.

Rossi won the title the following year and then paved the way for a grand prix entry by being crowned 125cc Italian champion, on similar machinery to that raced in the 125cc World Championship, in 1995.

Rossi's world championship debut came at the season-opening 1996 125cc Malaysian Grand Prix, where the 17-year-old qualified 13th before steering his Aprilia up to sixth place in the race. Having taken his first grand prix podium with third at round ten in Austria, Rossi claimed a debut victory – from pole position – next time out in the Czech Republic Grand Prix at Brno. The Italian went on to finish his first world championship season ninth overall.

With a season under his belt, and in a sign of things to come, Rossi utterly demolished the opposition in 1997 – winning eleven of the 15 races to be crowned the youngest ever 125cc world champion. Rossi graduated to the 250cc class the following season, again with Aprilia. The #46 repeated his 125cc form by winning during his rookie season – in which he finished second in

Above from left: 125cc Czech GP 1996. Rossi took his first ever World Championsip win at Brno.

Valentino and dad, Graziano Rossi, a Grand Prix winner himself, pictured with his son at the British Grand Prix, Donington Park, 1997.

Rossi celebrates his 125cc World Championship victory, at the Czech GP, Brno, 1997

Below: Valentino, leads Capirossi and Ukawa on his way to victory in the 250cc 1999 British Grand Prix.

Opposite page: Rossi, with tri-colour hairdo, at Imola 1998.

"When I went inside all the 100,000 fans went quiet, then when I came back out the noise was incredible!"

Above: Rossi celebrates his 250cc win at the Spanish Grand Prix in Jerez, 1999.

Below, from left: Valentino celebrates his first ever 500cc win at the British Grand Prix, Donington Park, 2000.

With Loris Capirossi and Garry McCoy on the podium, Malaysia 2001.

Rossi on his way to winning the first ever MotoGP race, the Japanese Grand Prix at Suzuka 2002.

Opposite page from left: A sea of Rossi fans in signal yellow.

Rossi, wins the Italian MotoGP at Mugello, 2003.

Rossi and Melandri on the podium after the Dutch MotoGP TT, 2004.

the championship – then took the title in style at his second attempt, scoring nine wins.

The 1999 season also saw the one of Rossi's most famous victory celebrations, when the Italian – whose popular post-race antics had been getting steadily more adventurous – darted into a trackside toilet for a joke 'comfort break' during the slow down lap at the Spanish Grand Prix.

"I saw the loo before the race and it looked strange – one toilet on its own by the side of the track – so I decided to go in it if I won," said Rossi. "When I went inside all the 100,000 fans went quiet, then when I came back out the noise was incredible!"

After a stellar record in the 125 and 250cc classes, Rossi hit the big time when he signed to ride for Honda in the 500cc World Championship, the pinnacle of motorcycle racing, for 2000. Some doubted Rossi could master the mega-powerful 500cc machines as he had the 125 and 250cc bikes, and he failed to finish his first race, but Rossi bounced back with a podium at round four, then his first premier-class victory at round nine, the British Grand Prix. Another win followed and Rossi finished the season a brilliant second in the championship – between Kenny Roberts Jr and arch-rival Max Biaggi.

When Rossi arrived in the 125cc World Championship, Biaggi was dominating the 250cc class - where he won four world titles – and Max remained one class ahead of Rossi until the #46 also reached 500cc in 2000. By then, a personality clash between the relaxed Rossi and intense Roman was well developed, enthusiastically fuelled by the Italian media – setting the scene for a bitter showdown.

Although Rossi got the upper hand over Biaggi during his superb debut 500cc season, the real action between them came in 2001, when the pair fought directly for the final 500cc world title before the new four-stroke MotoGP era. It didn't take long for the fireworks to ignite: At the very first race of the year Biaggi elbowed Rossi off the track as he tried to pass the Yamaha rider along Suzuka's fast main straight. Rossi kept control and fought his way back up to successfully pass Biaggi – then gave him the middle finger to illustrate his disgust!

By the time of the Catalan GP, round six, Rossi had won three races and Biaggi just one, but Biaggi was close on points due to Rossi's fall at the wet Italian GP – taking the tension between them to new heights.

When Rossi charged back from a poor start to beat Biaggi for victory in Barcelona it proved too much and, in the cramped confines of the staircase that led to the podium, a scuffle broke out between the two – leaving Biaggi with a small cut on his face. The pair were warned about their conduct by the FIM president and forced to shake hands in front of the press next time out in Holland, but it was far from sincere.

Back on track and Rossi continued to control the championship until a lowly seventh place at the German Grand Prix, combined with Biaggi's second victory of the year, saw the Roman suddenly jump to within 10 points of Valentino. The pressure was on, but Rossi regrouped over the summer break and hounded Biaggi for victory next time out at Brno, a circuit where Biaggi had been devastatingly successful in the past.

Something had to give and Biaggi fell while under pressure from his young opponent – leaving Rossi to cruise to his sixth victory of the season. When Rossi again won, and Biaggi again fell, next time out in Portugal, it became a question of when Rossi would lift the crown.

The 22-year-old ultimately became only the second rider in history, alongside Phil Read, to have won the 125, 250 and 500cc World Championships when he clinched the 2001 title two rounds early in Australia.

Honda then got the jump on its rivals, including Biaggi's Yamaha team, during the first year of the new MotoGP era in 2002 – when Rossi and his new RC211V motorcycle won eleven of the 16 races – allowing the Rossi/Biaggi rivalry to fade, helped partly by the emergence of Sete Gibernau.

Unlike with Biaggi, Rossi and Gibernau were initially friends, but when Gibernau became Valentino's nearest world championship contender their relationship soon began to cool under the pressure of a title fight – and eventually reached sub zero.

Following Daijiro Kato's tragic death after an accident at the 2003 Suzuka season opener, Gresini Honda team-mate

Gibernau was propelled into the spotlight – and responded with a dream victory next time out in South Africa. Rossi was genuinely pleased for the Spaniard and the pleasant attitude between the pair continued until Gibernau poached a painful last turn victory from the Repsol Honda rider at the German Grand Prix, round nine of the championship. That win marked Gibernau's fourth victory of 2003, confirming him as the new man of the moment, but tension grew between the title rivals due to their different level of status within Honda.

Rossi became increasingly sensitive to any suggestions that he had a machinery advantage over Gibernau, claiming there was little difference between their bikes, and was even rumoured to have considered riding Gibernau's RCV to prove it.

Regardless, Rossi stamped out Gibernau's challenge with six wins from the remaining seven races, but – despite winning his third premier-class title in a row – Rossi's relationship with Honda was beyond repair and he stunned the motorcycling world by signing for Yamaha, a team that had taken just one podium finish during 2003.

Rossi had been increasingly unhappy that his success was being attributed to superior machinery and intended to prove that it was the rider who makes the difference.

The 2004 season thus became known as 'Rossi vs. Honda' (led by Gibernau and Biaggi) and was one of the most anticipated seasons in the history of the sport.

Rossi wasted no time in taking the fight to his former employer, winning a breathtaking showdown with Biaggi at the South African season opener. Gibernau subsequently emerged as the strongest Honda rider, but a further eight victories for Rossi handed Yamaha its first 500cc/MotoGP title for 12 years and elevated the Italian's status to new heights.

Hostilities between Rossi and Gibernau had reached an all-time low during the closing stages of the season when, at the Qatar Grand Prix, Rossi was demoted to the back of the grid after his team was 'caught' cleaning his grid spot the night before the race.

Rightly or wrongly, Rossi blamed Gibernau for the 'unsporting' protest and, after the race, furiously declared that Gibernau 'would not win again'. Rossi's curse, as it became known, has so far not been lifted.

"After Qatar, whenever I saw Gibernau ahead of me I wanted to overtake him," Rossi admitted.

Rossi proved those weren't just hollow words at the season-opening 2005 Spanish Grand Prix at Jerez, Gibernau's home race. Rossi and Gibernau were locked together throughout, with Gibernau passing Rossi for the lead just a few corners from the finish. Rossi, typically refusing to admit defeat, then launched a 'do or die' move by diving for the inside at the final turn; the pair collided and Gibernau was forced off track, while Rossi took the win.

The podium ceremony marked the first and only time that Rossi has been booed by the fans, but he remained defiant. "We were fighting for an important victory, the fight was very hard throughout and at the end, for sure, there was a hard pass but – from my point of view – it was no more than that," stated Rossi. Gibernau and Rossi battled for victory many more times that season, but Rossi always got the better of the Spaniard who – like Biaggi before him – increasingly seemed burnt out by the pressure of fighting Valentino.

Rossi's third season at Yamaha, in 2006, was expected to be no less spectacular than the previous two years, but the latest YZR-M1 had unexpected technical problems that even Rossi couldn't overcome.

Accidents, injuries and plain bad luck compounded his misery, but a determined fightback during the strong half of the season – combined with a shock accident for title leader Nicky Hayden at the penultimate round – saw the Italian back in charge of the championship heading into the Valencian finale.

When Rossi qualified on pole position, a sixth MotoGP title looked a formality – but Rossi stunned the sell-out crown by falling during the race, handing Hayden the crown Rossi had owned since 2001.

After so much success, many were curious as to how Rossi would react to defeat, but when he reached out and shook the American's hand on the slowdown lap it was clear he felt no bitterness towards his former team-mate.

"All I can say is a big 'congratulations' to Nicky because he is a great guy, a great rider and he is the world champion because he has been the best this year," said Rossi. "I have known him a long time, I know his family well and even though I am disappointed I am also very happy for them. It has been a great fight with him this year – not like in the past with other riders when there have always been some polemics – and we have great respect for each other."

Above from left: Valentino behind his shades at the Australian MotoGP 2005.

Rossi kept up his run of wins in his home race the Italian MotoGP Race 2006.

Rossi overtakes Stoner in the Dutch TT MotoGP race, 2007.

Rossi, Wales Rally GB 2008.
Photograph: Photo4/Crashpa.Net

Opposite page: Rossi in action in Malaysia 2008.

The 2007 season marked the arrival of smaller 800cc engines and, after successful pre-season tests, Rossi began the year as the overwhelming favourite – only to be brought down to earth with a bump when Ducati's new signing Casey Stoner stormed to victory on his powerful Desmosedici in the opening round.

Rossi won next time out, but when Stoner took the next two victories it was clear that a new title rival had arrived to take on The Doctor – and that Ducati/Bridgestone had adapted much better to the new regulations than Yamaha/Michelin

Stoner's charge took him to ten wins and a debut world championship, while Rossi slumped to a MotoGP worst of third in the championship after a technical failure at the final Valencia round.

Adding to Rossi's frustration was that he had chosen to ride through the pain of a fractured right hand, sustained in a huge qualifying fall, to try and secure the single point he needed at Valencia to wrap-up the runner-up position behind Stoner. Although Rossi fell often at the start of his career, Valencia 2007 marked only the second time that Rossi had been badly injured. The first occasion was during practice for the 2006 Dutch TT when Rossi fractured his left foot and right wrist but, as at Valencia, bravely rode through the pain on race day. Indeed, Rossi has not missed a race since his 1996 debut.

Due to the obvious dangers, it's easy for the casual observer to dismiss Rossi and his fellow MotoGP racers as 'crazy' or assume they are simply unaware of the risks they face. However, Rossi believes that all good riders feel scared – and that fear is an essential ingredient of success.

"I think every clever rider is scared. This is because our sport is dangerous and fear is important to understand the limit – to stay quite near the limit but never go too much," he said.

After back-to-back defeats in 2006 and 2007 Rossi had demanded big changes from Yamaha and the first casualty was Michelin. After tyre problems during both seasons Rossi was determined to take on Stoner with the same Bridgestone rubber in 2008 and a deal with the Japanese manufacturer was eventually agreed, while Yamaha responded with a far more effective YZR-M1.

Stoner provided stiff resistance, but a pivotal mid-season victory by Rossi at Laguna Seca seemed to shake Stoner's confidence and the Australian fell from the lead of the next two races. Rossi took full advantage and finished the year with nine wins and 16 podiums from the 18 races, and an eighth world championship safely in the bag.

As a reward for regaining his MotoGP crown, Rossi was invited to test for the Ferrari Formula One team – with whom he had come close to making a full time F1 switch in 2006.

Rossi's 'secret' debut for the Italian team showed impressive potential and led to a series of further tests for the legendary Italian team – and intense speculation that he would quit two wheels for four. However, Rossi announced at the 2006 Italian Grand Prix that he had turned Ferrari down and would stay in MotoGP.

"I really thought about going," Rossi admitted. "I had a great test in Fiorano, about a second off the lap record, and that made the decision difficult. Then I went to Valencia and drove alongside the other F1 drivers, experiencing the atmosphere and the media pressure, and I made my decision."

Rossi's return to a Ferrari cockpit in late 2008 once again generated huge publicity, although this time without the pressure of a possible full time switch.

"To try the Ferrari again was a great emotion. I was fast, so I was happy; I am fast enough also in Formula One!" said Rossi, who lapped within 1.5sec of F1 pace before rain arrived. "In 2006 I decided to stay with the bike and, of course, I still have some doubts, but just to climb inside the red car at Mugello and work with Ferrari was fantastic."

Rossi then seemed to officially rule out a future F1 move: "I had my chance and I decided to stay with bikes. The choice is made and I don't think that there will be another possibility."

John Surtees is the only person to have won a world championship in both Formula One and Motorcycle Grand Prix racing.

No sooner had Rossi stepped out of the Ferrari F1 car than he was preparing for another kind of four-wheel adventure – at the wheel of a World Rally Car. Rossi has been driving rally cars for many years – resulting in a doomed entry in the 2002 Rally of Great Britain, where he crashed out after just 17 kilometres, but the Italian finished a creditable eleventh on his WRC return in the 2006 Rally of New Zealand.

2008 saw Rossi make a second attempt at the ultra-tough British WRC round, where he was a cautious 45th after stage one, before rising to 24th by the end of day one, 15th by the end of day two and twelfth at the completion of the 19th and final stage.

Valentino has a contract to race for Yamaha in 2009 and 2010, but has indicated that rallying will play a major part in his post-MotoGP future.

"I have always loved rally, ever since I was little," he said. "It is one of my great passions and it is great to do one when I have the time and the chance. I always enjoy it a lot and probably, when I have given up the bikes, I will do more... but it's not a close future, because I still want to race with the bike for a few more years!"

In addition to his F1 and WRC appearances, Rossi has also driven Mika Hakkinen's DTM Mercedes, appeared in a Maserati MC12 sports car and performed admirably against a karting world champion during a televised duel.

Intensely superstitious, Rossi has always raced with the #46 previously used by his father – shunning the #1 plate he has often been entitled to – and performs the same stretching ritual alongside his motorcycle before climbing aboard.

Rossi has broken several of motorcycle grand prix racing's most important records, although several are still to be claimed.

Of Rossi's 98 victories to date, 71 have been in the premier-class – more than any other rider in history. However Rossi is still two titles short of Giacomo Agostini's all-time record of eight 500cc World Championships.

Rossi also sits second to Agostini in terms of race wins in all grand prix classes (122) while his eight world titles in all classes is the fifth highest haul behind Mike Hailwood and Carlo Ubbiali (9), Angel Nieto (13) and Agostini (15).

"Agostini's record [122 wins] is something very important, naturally. I am not far off, but to do it I would have to continue to fight and race for a few more years!" said Rossi. "My principal objective is to win a few more world champion-ships; this is more important than catching Agostini. Obviously, if I succeed then it will be wonderful!

"2008 was difficult because it was the year in which I had to give the most of myself in order to win. In 2009 it will be even more difficult because my adversaries, who suffered in 2008, are now out for payback and will be looking to beat me. I think it's going to be even harder than 2008!" he said of the forthcoming season.

In contrast to his larger-than-life MotoGP persona, Rossi keeps a low profile away from the racetrack, and gives away little about his private life.

However, he admits to being a passionate supporter of the Inter Milan football team and is good friends with the team's Italian international Marco Materazzi. Valentino often takes his summer holidays at the party island of Ibiza and spends large parts of the winter break snowboarding. Rossi, who struggles with early morning starts, is also a dog lover, and carried a sticker of his pet bulldog Guido on his motorcycle.

When Rossi turned 30 on February 16, 2009 he received birthday wishes from the likes of Hollywood stars Tom Cruise and Daniel Day-Lewis. "Valentino, you are a true champion," wrote Cruise. "You keep raising the bar, relentlessly pursuing the next race, the next challenge, the next championship... I, like countless others, know that when you're on the track anything is possible."

Rossi has used several nicknames during his career: The first, 'Rossifumi', was a tribute to wild Japanese racer Norifumi Abe and was followed by 'Valentinik', based on a cartoon character.

In the premier class, Rossi settled on 'The Doctor', to reflect his level of expertise on the racetrack. The nickname was given official weight in 2005, when Rossi received an honorary doctorate in communications from the University of Urbino. Rossi's helmet designs traditionally feature the sun and moon, to reflect the contrasting sides of his personality, and incorporate his favourite colour, yellow.

Rossi, who remains single, retuned to live in Italy after reaching a settlement with the Italian tax authorities in early 2008 and now operates as his own manager. His best friend, Uccio Salucci, works as his personal assistant in the MotoGP paddock.

Valentino's desire to win remains as strong as ever, and having to settle for second place finishes in the opening two rounds of the 2009 season, merely strengthened his resolve. Rossi's performance in the Spanish Grand Prix – in which he overtook his three main title rivals to win – underlined his steely determination to remain at the very top for the foreseeable future...

"2008 was difficult because it was the year in which I had to give the most of myself in order to win"

TWIST

Rossi's flambouyant personality, exotic appearance and electrifying riding style combined to make him the popular rookie of the year in any class.

18/08/1996
CZECH GRAND PRIX

Valentino Rossi took his first-ever grand prix victory by just 0.245sec from fellow Aprilia rider Jorge Martinez at the 1996 125cc Czech Republic Grand Prix at Brno. It was Rossi's eleventh grand prix start. Rossi, who had taken his first podium at the previous round in Austria, finished his first season in GP racing ninth in the world championship with one win, two podiums and one pole position.

1997

125cc CHAMPION

'ROSSIFUMI'

13/04/1997

MALAYSIAN GRAND PRIX

Valentino Rossi began his second season in grand prix racing by winning the opening round in Malaysia. After a classic battle, Rossi took victory by almost one second from Kazuto Sakata of Japan.

04/05/1997

SPANISH GRAND PRIX

Rossi crashed out of round two of the 1997 125cc World Championship, in Japan. *"I thought I could win,' he said later. "Now I just think I am an idiot."* But he bounced back with victory during the first European round of the year at Jerez in Spain. Fifteenth after the first lap, he surged through. *"Passing people as though he had a special dispensation from law of physics, an extra 50cc, or an indecent amount of talent."*

18/05/1997

ITALIAN GRAND PRIX

Rossi took his first grand prix victory in front of his home Italian fans at round four of the 1997 season. Rossi's #46 machine crossed the finish line a confident 3.311sec clear of the veteran Jorge Martinez.

Showing a maturity beyond his years, Valentino had toyed with the opposition, changing the pace of the race to break the challenge of his opponents.

Rossi's victory was consumate: a brilliant tactical race.

08/06/1997
FRENCH GRAND PRIX

After missing out on his third race victory in a row by just 0.004sec to Noboru Ueda in Austria, Rossi returned to the top with a 2.961sec win over Tomomi Manako at the following French Grand Prix. In a sign of bigger celebrations to come, Rossi wore a Jester's hat on the podium.

Assen is the only circuit from the original 1949 world championship which still holds a motorcycle grand prix. Rossi took his first victory at the legendary Dutch track with a tight 0.1sec victory over Manako on a day when the top five riders were covered by less than one second! Valentino celebrated his achievement by donning a Superman inspired Superfumi cape on his slowing-down lap.

Rossi risked everything under braking to snatch a brilliant victory on the final lap.

IMOLA GRAND PRIX

On top of the world. Rossi took his second win of the season on Italian asphalt with a 1.6sec victory over Manako at Imola, to maintain a healthy lead in the 125cc World Championship.

Rossi's found firm friendships with Japanese riders such as Takuma Aoki. At races he was also a regular visitor to the press room, where he cultivated the Italian press to ensure himself plenty of media exposure.

20/07/1997
GERMAN GRAND PRIX

Rossi's world championship ambitions were underlined when he made it a perfect three wins in a row – from three pole positions – at the German Grand Prix. The rain-affected race looked likely to fall to Kazuto Sakata, who held a commanding lead until his Aprilia's engine seized. Valentino crossed the line just ahead of the Yamaha of Yoshiaki Katoh *(main picture)*.

03/08/1997
RIO GRAND PRIX

The Rio Grand Prix may have seen Rossi's pole run end, but the young Italian kept his victory stretch intact with a 1.4sec triumph over Ueda. Third placed Youichi Ui was a further seven seconds behind.

17/08/1997

BRITISH GRAND PRIX

Another thrilling 125cc race was decided on the final corner after Tomomi Manako failed to force his bike inside Rossi's and clattered to the ground. Valentino thus made it six wins in a row, and – having decided Donington Park was near enough to Nottingham – dressed up as Robin Hood for the podium ceremony!

31/08/1997
CZECH GRAND PRIX

One year after his first grand prix victory, Rossi secured his first world championship with a close third place finish at Brno. The achievement made Rossi the youngest ever 125cc world champion, but wasn't an easy ride for the Italian, who was unhappy with the set up of his bike. The Hondas of Ueda and Manako had the legs on his Aprilia, but third place was good enough to claim the title.

The last lap was one of Rossi's best of the season.

14/09/1997
CATALAN GRAND PRIX

Rossi celebrated his world title by romping to a six-second victory over Sakata at Catalunya. The win was Rossi's tenth of the season.

28/09/1997
INDONESIAN GRAND PRIX

Rossi's final victory of the 1997 season came with another confident win over Sakata, this time at the penultimate round in Indonesia.

His latest podium jape was the wearing of a joke-shop head bandage – a reference to his concussion after being a passenger in a car (crashed by his father Graziano!) back in Italy the previous weekend.

Valentino could only manage sixth place in his final 125cc race, in Australia, but still finished the year with 11 wins from 15 races and 13 podium finishes.

A young Valentino, with one of his heroes, Barry Sheene.

1998

DUTCH TT

Rossi took his first ever 250cc victory at round seven at Assen. Valentino stormed to a massive 19sec victory over fellow Aprilia rider Jurgen Fuchs, who just edged out the Honda of Haruchika Aoki.

ROSSIFUMI

06/09/1998

IMOLA GRAND PRIX

Rossi rode a special patriotically-coloured Aprilia to his second 250cc victory at round eleven, held at Imola. Rossi beat Capirossi by 2.7sec with Stefano Perugini completing an all-Italian podium in third.

Rossi took a home win, in full showman heaven, with bike, helmet, leathers and even hair painted in the Italian tri-colour.

20/09/1998
CATALAN GRAND PRIX

Rossi beat championship contenders - and official Aprilia riders - Harada and Capirossi to take his second victory in as many starts. The race is best remembered for Rossi's victory celebration, which saw him take a huge mock chicken around the racetrack on the slowdown lap!

Did Rossi earn approval or punishment when he gave a man in a hen suit a lift on his victory lap? Apparently neither. "It is forbidden to carry a passenger, but the rules say nothing about chickens," said an official.

"I was riding smoothly and carefully in the early laps after my bad start, and only overtaking where it was really safe. I think it shows I'm more mature now."

04/10/1998
AUSTRALIAN GRAND PRIX

"When Tetsuya crashed, I thought that second would be OK for Loris and the championship, and I could try to win."

The chicken meets the penguin. Rossi kept his winning streak alive by taking his first ever Phillip Island victory from Capirossi and Honda's Olivier Jacque. However, Rossi's early season accidents meant he was already out of the world championship battle.

Rossi completed an incredible end-of-season run by taking his fourth victory in a row during a race that saw a controversial last lap clash between title rivals Loris Capirossi and Tetsuya Harada.

With Harada failing to finish, Rossi concluded his first season of 250cc competition second in the championship behind fellow countryman Capirossi.

25/10/1998
ARGENTINE GRAND PRIX

1999

250cc CHAMPION

09/05/1999

SPANISH GRAND PRIX

After finishing fifth and seventh in the opening rounds, it was a case of third time lucky for Rossi as he took his first victory of the season at Jerez in Spain. Rossi moved swiftly from third to first, and then held off future MotoGP team-mate Tohru Ukawa by a comfortable 4.4sec at the flag.

After winning, the ever-theatrical Rossi stunned the 100,000 fans with one of his most famous post-race celebrations – the Italian darting into a trackside toilet!

06/06/1999

ITALIAN GRAND PRIX

Rossi won his first 250cc Italian Grand Prix by fighting his way forward from sixth on the grid. Rossi went on to win by 2.6sec while Ukawa and Ralf Waldmann were separated by just 0.041sec in second and third places. Despite his second victory of the year, Rossi was only third in the world championship standings, 31 points behind Ukawa.

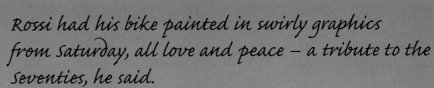

Rossi had his bike painted in swirly graphics from Saturday, all love and peace – a tribute to the seventies, he said.

20/06/1999

CATALAN GRAND PRIX

Rossi increased the pressure on championship leader Ukawa with a close 0.258sec victory over the Honda rider at Catalunya. Ukawa and Rossi battled throughout the race the Japanese rider harrying Rossi first one side and then the other as they entered the final lap. Rossi said later he'd slowed the pace to try and get Ukawa to lead again *"but he wouldn't do it. Then I tried as hard as I could for a few laps, but when I looked round he was still there. So on the last lap I kept all the doors closed."*

04/07/1999

BRITISH GRAND PRIX

Having lost out to Capirossi at the Dutch TT, Rossi got back to winning ways at the following race the, British Grand Prix, at Donington Park. Rossi initially led the 250cc race but when spots of rain threatened, as the leader he raised his hand to halt proceedings on lap nine. The envisaged downpour never appeared however, and Valentino saw off the challenge of Capirossi to win the second part of the race by 1.5 seconds. Ukawa finished fourth and was now just seven points in front of Valentino in the championship.

After the Sachsenring race, Rossi, was hot property – with the offer of a 500cc works Honda for 2000.

18/07/1999

GERMAN GRAND PRIX

Rossi took the lead of the 1999 250cc World Championship at round nine in Germany, when he won his fifth race of the season by 0.148sec from Capirossi. The pair had another torrid race long battle and Valentino saw off yet another desperate last lap attack from his rival, the duelling pair having pulled almost nine seconds clear of third-placed Waldmann. Ukawa failed to finish, handing Rossi the title advantage by 18 points.

22/08/1999
CZECH REPUBLIC GRAND PRIX

Rossi scored his third win in a row with a last lap pass on Waldmann at Brno. With Capirossi's race compromised by a down on power engine, it was the German Aprilia rider who took the fight to Valentino. His challenge was a spirited one, and if it were not for gearshift problems, he might have prevailed. As it was, Valentino grabbed the initiative to win by just over half a second. Ukawa was third, thus Rossi's championship lead increased to 27 points.

On the bike, Rossi is both gangling and adventurous given to finding different corner lines when need be, finding and using the best of his Aprilia's special characteristics.

10/10/1999
SOUTH AFRICAN GRAND PRIX

Rossi put one hand on the 250cc World Championship with victory from sixth on the grid in South Africa. Rossi dropped back to eighth on lap one, but climbed quickly back up the order and took the lead from Ukawa with seven laps to go. Ukawa faded to fourth in the closing stages, leaving him 47 points behind Rossi with just two races and 50 points remaining.

03/10/1999
AUSTRALIAN GRAND PRIX

Despite finishing second and eighth in the two rounds prior to Phillip Island, Rossi had only lost one point to Ukawa heading to Australia, where the Italian again underlined his immense talent by winning out after a four-way battle involving Tohru Ukawa, Shinya Nakano and Olivier Jacque.

Showing his precocious class Valentino upped his speed while also holding tight lines to keep all doors closed in notching a 0.103sec victory over Olivier Jacque. Third for Ukawa meant Rossi could head for the final three rounds a healthy 35 points clear of the Japanese rider.

24/10/1999

RIO GRAND PRIX

Above: Man on a mission: Rossi leads rivals Tohru Ukawa and Loris Capirossi on the way to the title.

Top left: Battle of the hairstyles, Valentino with 125cc star Marco Melandri.

VALENTINIK

Rossi claimed his first and only 250cc World Championship in perfect style with victory at the penultimate round in Rio.

Slow off the line saw him plummet from second on the grid to twelfth at the end of lap one, but he soon picked off West, Vincent and McWilliams. *"Then I had a clear track and I could go faster to come back to the top group."*

Valentino then charged his way forwards to dispute the lead on lap eight. After trailing Ukawa for five laps Rossi really showed his class in forcing his way to the front and pulling clear by 1.3sec at the finish line.

It was the Italian's ninth win of the season and he became the first 250cc World Champion to be crowned under the age of 21 (Mike Hailwood was 21 when he was the 1961 250cc champion).

02/04/2000
MALAYSIAN GRAND PRIX

Rossi moved from Aprilia to Honda for his debut season in the premier 500cc class, and initially found the huge power increase tough to tame. Valentino crashed out of his first two races, in Africa and Malaysia (pictured), but proved speed was no problem by qualifying in the top seven at both events.

Rossi moved into second at the end of lap 4, only to crash much as he had in South Africa with too much corner speed and too much angle of lean...

09/07/2000
BRITISH GRAND PRIX

Rossi won his first 500GP on a drying track at Donington Park (round nine). Starting from fourth, Rossi slumped to eleventh on the opening lap but caught race leaders Kenny Roberts Jr and Jeremy McWilliams by the midway point. The trio battled to the finish, with Rossi winning by 0.395sec from Roberts with McWilliams also less than a second from victory. *"I am very happy. It was very hard to beat Jeremy and my tyre was finished,"* said Rossi.

2000

RIO GRAND PRIX

Rossi's first dry-weather 500 win was achieved with total assurance

Rossi's second and final victory of his rookie 500cc season came at round 14 in Rio. Rossi took the lead at the midway stage then held off a determined attack from home hero Alex Barros to cross the line almost one second in front of the Brazilian. *"It was a very important win,"* said Rossi. However, sixth place for Roberts Jr was enough to secure the world championship with two rounds still to go. With podium placings in the final two races of the season, Rossi finished the season 49 points behind the Suzuki rider, in second position.

Left: Pause for thought on the podium as Alex Barros (far left) Rossi and Garry McCoy are presented with their trophies.

Rossi claimed Honda's 500th motorcycle grand prix win at the opening round of the 2001 season, during a race that saw a heated exchange with arch-rival Max Biaggi. Rossi caught fourth placed Biaggi early in the race and tried to ride around the outside as they accelerated onto the home straight. Biaggi elbowed Rossi onto the grass, but Rossi made the move stick shortly after – and signalled his displeasure with a 'one fingered' wave! Rossi then took the race lead on lap seven and eventually won by 0.7sec from Garry McCoy.

2001

08/04/2001

JAPANESE GRAND PRIX

500cc CHAMPION

Rossi was now styled "The Doctor", the latest twist in his relentless self-publicity.

22/04/2001

SOUTH AFRICAN GRAND PRIX

Rossi took his first ever 500cc pole position in South Africa, and converted it into a race victory by just 0.660sec from Capirossi at the end of 28 thrilling laps of the Welkom circuit. After some superlative racing, Rossi's second straight win was no runaway, but achieved with a string of consecutive lap records in the closing laps under severe pressure from his near namesake Capirossi. The older rider was also breaking the record. Just never quite as much as Rossi, who fastest lap was the last, and he still only won by six-tenths. It was a victory of great assurance all the same.

Valentino's perfect start to the season placed him 22 points clear of a Capirossi in the world championship standings. His somewhat disgruntled opponent complaining about the lack of parity in their Hondas.

THE DOCTOR

06/05/2001

SPANISH GRAND PRIX

Rossi's flawless run continued at the first European round, in Spain, where he won by 2.3sec from Norick Abe after a race long battle *(below)* with the Yamaha rider. Rossi's title lead had now risen to 31 points over new nearest rival Abe.

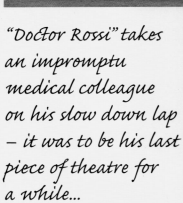

"Doctor Rossi" takes an impromptu medical colleague on his slow down lap – it was to be his last piece of theatre for a while...

ITALIAN GRAND PRIX

Rossi unveiled a special Hawaiian livery for his home Italian Grand Prix, but after qualifying on pole, was caught out by wet conditions during the restarted second half of the race. *"This has been a movie rather than a race but without a happy ending,"* said Rossi, who crashed out of second place on the very last lap. The superstitious Rossi has never used a special livery at the Italian GP since. The accident reduced Rossi's championship lead to 21 points over Biaggi after five rounds.

Rossi bounced back from his Mugello nightmare with victory from pole next time out in Catalunya. Rossi was only twelfth at the end of lap one but took the lead from Capirossi halfway through the 25 lap race. Biaggi later relegated Capirossi a further position but was now 26 points from Rossi in the championship. After the race, and out of sight of the TV cameras, Rossi and Biaggi exchanged blows on the way up to the podium!

BRITISH GRAND PRIX

Another masterful performance from the 22-year old, showing a precocious racecraft beyond his years.

Rossi delivered one of his best 500cc rides so far at the 2001 British Grand Prix, when he overcame a 200km/h practice crash - and eleventh place on the grid - to take the race lead from Biaggi on lap 18 of the 30 lap race. **"I think that was my best and most difficult race in 500s,"** said an ecstatic Rossi, who won by 1.8sec. With half of the 16 rounds complete, Rossi's title advantage stood at 26 points over Biaggi.

CZECH REPUBLIC GRAND PRIX

Brno was a pivotal race in terms of the world championship. Biaggi had closed to within 10 points of Rossi after victory in Germany and boasted a formidable record in the Czech Republic. But Rossi dug deep, clinging to Biaggi for the first half of the race and was then handed victory when Biaggi fell as he tried to shake off the #46. Biaggi's mistake put Rossi's title lead back up to 29 points. ***"It was a very difficult and very important race,"*** said Rossi.

"The turning point of my season was Brno. After that race, we were back on track."

09/09/2001

PORTUGUESE GRAND PRIX

If Biaggi's title chances were dealt a heavy blow in Brno, they received
a mortal wound next time out in Portugal – when Rossi once again
won and Biaggi once again fell. Biaggi had qualified on pole, but was
overtaken early in the race by Rossi and then fell from third with six laps
to go. Biaggi recovered to fifth, but had slipped 43 points behind Rossi.
*"This victory is very important for the championship with Max
crashing,"* said Rossi.

07/10/2001

PACIFIC GRAND PRIX

Rossi's eighth victory of the 2001 season came at Motegi in Japan, where 'The Doctor' administered a 2.6sec win over Alex Barros while Biaggi's slim title chances all but ended when he fell for the third time in four races. Max tumbled from the lead on lap six, leaving Rossi to lead the rest of the race and take a 67 point lead into the final three rounds, with only 75 points still available.

"Congratulations to Rossi, who has been good, smart and clever to use at the best what he has in his hands."

Max Biaggi

"My best win of the season – probably of my career – was in Australia. I knew the World Championship was at stake and I only had to finish in the top eight, but I took the risk and the satisfaction was enormous."

14/10/2001
AUSTRALIAN GRAND PRIX

Rossi secured his first premier-class title, and the last ever 500cc crown, in thrilling style by claiming a nail-biting 0.013sec victory over Biaggi at Phillip Island. Rossi didn't need to beat Biaggi to wrap up the crown, and Valentino's willingness to sacrifice a 'safe' ride to try and win the race said everything about his character. Rossi and Biaggi exchanged the lead repeatedly and Rossi's victory pass came on the very final lap. ***"I knew the world championship was at stake but to win a race like this is really something,"*** said Rossi.

The title may have been decided, but Rossi continued his winning ways next time out at Sepang in Malaysia, when he took his tenth victory of the year by 3.6sec from Capirossi.

After winning the race, Valentino enthused. "In this heat, there's only one way to ride... spinning and sliding. It's big fun to ride a 500 like that."

RIO GRAND PRIX

Having won the last 500cc World Championship, Rossi concluded the season by winning the last ever 500cc Grand Prix. Valentino had been leading when rain forced the race to be stopped and, although Rossi was narrowly beaten by Checa during the restarted race, he was close enough to claim the win overall, helped when the pair were lapping Anthony West, who was running with a shredded rear tyre. Checa's momentum was checked, allowing Rossi to close in and take the victory by just 0.143sec on the combined race times.

"I pushed so hard that I nearly crashed a few times and when we finished the race I didn't know who had won," said Rossi.

Rossi's pre-season form led his compatriot Capirossi to say that he could win the championship with one hand tied behind his back...

JAPANESE GRAND PRIX

Valentino wrote his name into another piece of Motorcycle Grand Prix history by winning the first race of the new 990cc four-stroke MotoGP era, during round one of the 2002 season at a wet Suzuka. Rossi worked his way forwards from fifth on lap one, taking the lead from Akira Ryo late in the race and handing the new Honda RC211V a 1.6sec victory over the Suzuki wild-card. ***"This is an important win because it is the first MotoGP race, but also because it was raining and I didn't know how my machine would react,"*** said a relieved Rossi.

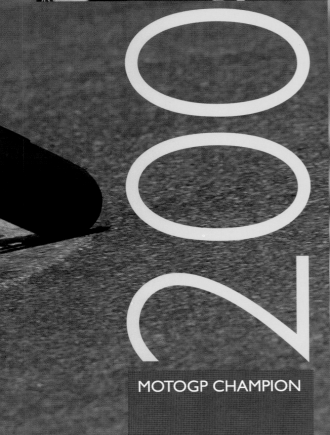

2002

MOTOGP CHAMPION

05/05/2002
SPANISH GRAND PRIX

Clutch problems causing wheelspin contributed to surprising defeat at the hands of team-mate Tohru Ukawa in South Africa, but Rossi resumed business as usual at Jerez. In front of 130,000 fans at he re-established control with a 1.2sec victory over Daijiro Kato, riding a 500cc Honda, but it was not an easy win.

On the second lap he was hit from behind by Kenny Roberts's Suzuki and all but crashed. It dropped him from third to ninth, forcing a stirring recovery ride. Jerez marked the start of seven successive race wins for Rossi.

19/05/2002
FRENCH GRAND PRIX

Rossi secured his third win of the season at Le Mans after taking the lead from Ukawa just one lap before the race was stopped early due to rain. *"It's 25 very important points, although it's not my favourite grand prix win,"* admitted Rossi, now leading Ukawa by 34 points in the championship.

Rossi understood the implications of the rain threat without any special pit signals...

02/06/2002

ITALIAN GRAND PRIX

Rossi scored his first premier-class win at his home Italian Grand Prix, when memories of the 2001 season were revived by a close duel with Biaggi, whose Yamaha had been no match for the RCVs during the early rounds. The Italian superstars broke away at the front, with Rossi then edging away from Biaggi to win by 2.4sec. After winning the race, Rossi was given a speeding ticket by some of his friends dressed as policemen!

Left: Home from home. Rossi installed in his pit a yellow foam armchair, but crew chief Jerry Burgess – tiring of the games and needing the space – threw it out after just one day without ceremony!

Right: Biaggi was content with his second place on the improving Yamaha, whilst Tohru Ukawa seems less than pleased to have finished some twelve seconds adrift of his victorious team mate.

Bottom: The adoration squads were out in force at Mugello as Rossi once again put on another piece of carefully orchestrated post-race theatre.

"It was a really hard race for the bike, the tyres – and for me."

CATALAN GRAND PRIX

Ukawa re-emerged to challenge Rossi at Catalunya and the Japanese was left just 0.88sec behind his fellow Repsol Honda rider at the chequered flag. *"When I was at the front I couldn't get away as the tyres were spent,"* explained Rossi.

With two laps left, Rossi finally used everything the V5 had to offer, blasting past on the front straight and pulling away with great assurance.

29/06/2002
DUTCH TT

Rossi won from pole at Assen, but faced a stiff challenge from Alex Barros, who put his 500cc two-stroke at the front of the field until Rossi made his move on lap 16 of 19. *"I was worried Alex might get away. I have never seen a 500cc two-stroke ridden as fast as that since 2000,"* admitted Rossi, who was 2.2sec in front of the Brazilian at the chequered flag.

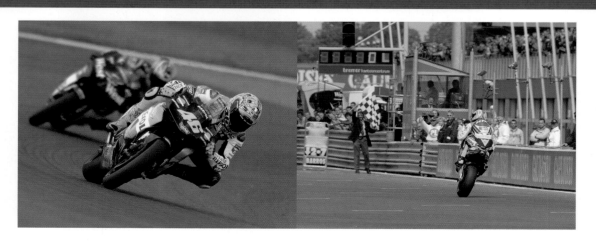

BRITISH GRAND PRIX

The first season of MotoGP reached its midway point at Donington Park, an event that was also Rossi's 100th grand prix start. The Italian marked the occasion by claiming his 46th Grand Prix win, having taken the lead when Checa fell just in front of him on lap 18. Rossi had now won 20 of his first 40 premier-class races and took a huge 87-point lead over Ukawa into the second half of the season.

GERMAN GRAND PRIX

Rossi's victory streak reached seven in Germany, but only after race leaders Alex Barros and Olivier Jacque – both riding 500cc two-strokes – collided just three laps from the end. ***"I saw Barros brake too deep, try to stop, but it was impossible. Jacque was unlucky, but the race was not finished because I had Biaggi and Ukawa close behind,"*** said Rossi, now 96 points clear of closest rival Ukawa.

Barros's ruinous attack on poor Jacques gifted the win to Rossi...

PORTUGUESE GRAND PRIX

Honda's perfect season had come to an end at the previous Brno round, when Rossi was forced out with a rear tyre problem – helping Biaggi claim the Yamaha M1's first ever win – but the #46 found luck back on his side at Estoril, when Suzuki's Sete Gibernau crashed out of the lead with four laps to go. ***"I'm happy for victory but so sorry for Sete,"*** said Rossi, whose 89-point lead meant he could claim the title next time out in Rio.

21/09/2002

RIO GRAND PRIX

Valentino became the first ever MotoGP world champion, with four rounds still to go, with his tenth victory of the season, in Rio. Rossi triumphed by 1.7sec over Biaggi in wet conditions, while an early race accident for Ukawa confirmed Rossi as champion. Rossi marked his latest world title with a World Cup themed celebration, a reference to new football world champion's Brazil. *"I am absolutely delighted with this victory and above all with my fourth world championship,"* smiled Rossi.

Rossi's race had been superb. His title was now unassailable. It had been a remarkable year. And it wasn't over yet...

Was it luck or skill that allowed Rossi to follow his usual line, missing his erstwhile rival's back wheel by what looked inches? Let's just call it superlative judgement and race maturity...

20/10/2002
AUSTRALIAN GRAND PRIX

After clinching the title, Rossi lost the next two races to Barros (now on a four-stroke) and Biaggi respectively, but returned to the top step of the podium at the penultimate round in Australia. Rossi got the better of Barros after an epic duel, which ended when the Brazilian ran off track on the last lap while trying to outbrake the Italian. The win was Rossi's eleventh and last of the season and his 50th in grand prix racing. *"50 victories is a dream,"* said Rossi. *"I'm very happy with this victory because Barros is very hard to race."*

2003

MOTOGP CHAMPION

Having run out of fuel post race, the victor hitches a ride back from Noriyuki Haga in time for the podium ceremonies.

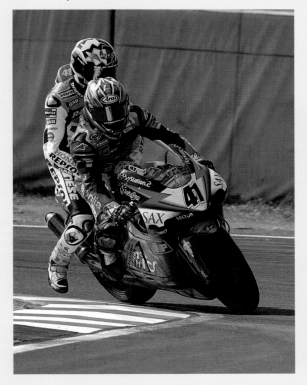

06/04/2003

JAPANESE GRAND PRIX

Valentino began his fourth season in the premier-class with his third victory in a row at Suzuka in Japan, but all thoughts were with Daijiro Kato, who suffered a serious accident during the race. Kato later died of his injuries. ***"Nothing about the race was important after hearing the news of Kato. I was shocked and greatly saddened,"*** said Rossi.

Italian trio. Rossi leads deadly rival Max Biaggi (now riding a similar Honda) and Loris Capirossi making his debut on the V4 Ducati Desmosedici.

11/05/2003
SPANISH GRAND PRIX

Kato's Gresini Honda team-mate Sete Gibernau had taken an emotional victory at round two in South Africa, but Rossi returned to the top step of the podium next time out at Jerez. Rossi was just ninth after some first turn mayhem, but fought his way forwards to snatch the lead on lap four, then eased away from nearest rival Biaggi by 6.3sec – thrilling the 128,000 fans with some huge slides in the process. Rossi now led Biaggi by 14 points.

Rossi's third win in five races was a typical masterstroke – but it would be his last for a while...

08/06/2003

ITALIAN GRAND PRIX

After being narrowly beaten by Gibernau in France, Rossi raised his game for his home fans at Mugello, where he won an all-Italian showdown with Capirossi and Biaggi. The trio battled relentlessly, with a jubilant Rossi finally triumphing by 1.4sec over Ducati rider Capirossi. In the championship, Rossi was now 32 points clear of Biaggi. Meanwhile, off track, the first rumours that Rossi could sensationally leave Honda at the end of the year began to emerge.

27/07/2003

GERMAN GRAND PRIX

After Mugello, Rossi suffered a slump – by his standards – losing the next four races (he was penalised after "winning" at Donington), culminating in a last turn defeat at the hands of Gibernau in Germany. *"I made a big mistake,"* confessed Rossi, who was leading into the last corner. *"I don't know why I went so tight into the final turn, but I thought Sete may go inside."*

After nine rounds, Rossi was leading Gibernau by 29 points, but the Spaniard had won four races compared with three for Rossi.

Rossi had suffered this accident in practice at the Sachsenring – it marked his only fall during the entire 2003 season!

17/08/2003

CZECH REPUBLIC GRAND PRIX

Rossi returned from the summer break with a point to prove and delivered one of his best performances at Brno, taking revenge on Gibernau by overtaking the Catalan on the final lap and hung on to win by just 0.04sec. *"We were fighting without tactics and without thinking, giving 100 percent and wanting to be at the front,"* said Rossi.

Rossi celebrated by dressing as a prisoner, a sign of how he now felt 'trapped' by his stunning success at Honda. It was another indication that Rossi would seek a new challenge in 2004.

07/09/2003
PORTUGUESE GRAND PRIX

Rossi kept Gibernau on the defensive, by winning next time out in Portugal, marking the first time in 2003 that any rider had won two races in a row. Rossi overcame early leader Biaggi during the middle stages on his way to a comprehensive victory. Gibernau was only fourth and had now slipped 46 points from Rossi.

Rossi had turned the corner and was rewriting the ground rules...

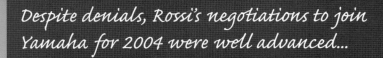

20/09/2003
RIO GRAND PRIX

Rossi made it three wins in a row with a convincing 3sec victory over Gibernau in Rio. The win was Valentino's 30th in the premier-class and handed Honda its third consecutive manufacturers' championship, with four rounds still to go. Rossi's title lead now stood at 51 points with 100 remaining.

Rossi was in a class of his own on at a difficult circuit. *"You need to be very gentle on the throttle because of the bumps and the low grip,"* Valentino explained, making it sound easy.

AUSTRALIAN GRAND PRIX

Rossi's third consecutive Phillip Island victory marked an unforgettable performance, since the Italian was forced to overcome a ten second penalty – to be added to his final race time – for overtaking under yellow flags early in the race. Rossi was informed via his pit board and set an astonishing pace to cross the finish line 15.2sec in front of nearest rival Capirossi.

"I closed my eyes for the last ten laps!" joked Rossi, who carried a #7 flag in memory of Barry Sheene. *"It was incredible. I've never ridden a whole race at 100 percent before."*

12/10/2003

MALAYSIAN GRAND PRIX

Rossi confirmed his third consecutive 500cc/MotoGP crown, and fifth world championship, with victory at Sepang, round 14 of 16. Rossi only had to finish second to Gibernau, but the Italian pursued the Spaniard mercilessly and took the lead on lap seven.

"This fifth title is like a dream," smiled Rossi. *"It was a very hard race just like the whole season but also very good fun. Sete put me under pressure but we've finished on the podium at every race this year and that's why we were able to win the title."*

Having won two Championships in a row with the dominant Honda RCV211, a fresh challenge lay elsewhere...

02/11/2003
VALENCIA GRAND PRIX

Peace, love and silly sixties wig – Rossi carried through the Austin Powers theme of his special last-race graphics for Honda.

Rossi finished the season with nine wins a record total of 357 points. He also finished every race on the podium.

VALENCIA GRAND PRIX

Rossi's final victory as a Honda rider came at the season-finale in Valencia, where he absorbed pressure from Gibernau for 25 of the 30 laps, before setting a record-breaking pace which the Catalan couldn't follow. Rossi, who rode in a special 'Austin Powers' livery, announced his departure from Honda that evening.

"It is true. Next year we don't race together," said Valentino. *"It's been an unforgettable four years and together we have won over 50% of the races. I cannot reveal which bike I will be riding next year, but I can say that it will be a big challenge – it maybe even seems a little crazy right now!"*

Rossi was later confirmed as a Yamaha rider. Yamaha had taken just one podium finish during the 2003 season, a third position by Barros at Le Mans.

18/04/2004

AFRICA'S GRAND PRIX

Rossi's Yamaha debut in the 2004 Africa's Grand Prix was one of the most anticipated events in modern motorcycling history - and it didn't disappoint: The race saw a stunning battle between Rossi and Biaggi (Honda), the two Italians pushing themselves to the limit as they exchanged the lead and pulled away from Gibernau.

Rossi was just half a bike length ahead of Biaggi as the last lap began and both rode the rest of the lap like their lives depended on it. Rossi absorbed the constant pressure to wheelie over the finish line with his fist in the air and claim Yamaha's first win since 2002 by just 0.210sec.

"This is the best race of my career, it's a real surprise for us, for everyone, and it's difficult to explain the emotion," said a stunned Rossi. *"I had a good fight with Biaggi. I was slower in some parts, faster in others but I knew I couldn't make any mistakes. After a race, when I win, usually I'm really happy but this time it was more and I had to stop for a moment to take it all in. It was fantastic!"*

Gibernau finished over seven seconds behind the race leaders, while Rossi's fellow Yamaha riders were just 9th, 10th and 11th – an average of 40-seconds slower than Rossi.

"Valentino really is a genius behind the bike," said Yamaha technical boss Masao Furusawa.

2004

MOTOGP CHAMPION

His gesture of leaving
dominant Honda to join
underdogs Yamaha was
sporting, defiant and
well-timed.

06/06/2004

ITALIAN GRAND PRIX

Rossi had finished fourth in the two races after Welkom, but returned to the podium with his third home win in a row at Mugello. Rossi won a six-lap dash by just 0.36sec from Gibernau, after the original thriller had been red flagged due to rain.

"It was like winning twice!" said Rossi, who rode with a mock wooden helmet in reference to his recent fourth places. *"The first race was in the dry, when it seemed like I made 30 or 40 overtaking manoeuvres. The new race was held in incredible conditions – slick tyres on a wet track. To win in front of all these people is fantastic. It's hard to explain the emotion I felt when I heard the crowds cheering for me on the last few laps."*

Rossi was now 10 points behind Gibernau in the world championship, with two wins each.

At a track that should have featured the faster Hondas, Rossi proved that the right rider can still prevail.

13/06/2004
CATALAN GRAND PRIX

Rossi scored an important victory over Gibernau during an intense Catalan Grand Prix duel. Rossi made his victory pass with two laps to go and reached the chequered flag just 0.159sec before Gibernau, who was born and raised in nearby Barcelona.

"To win at Mugello and Catalunya is like a dream because we knew they would be two difficult tracks for us with the long straights and the extra top speed of the Honda," beamed Rossi, who dressed up as a Doctor to celebrate his win.

Rossi's last-lap move was so daring it left Gibernau not only breathless, but also minus a few bits of bodywork

26/06/2004
DUTCH TT

Assen saw another thrilling Rossi/Gibernau duel, albeit one that almost turned nasty. Gibernau led the race until the last lap, when Rossi dived inside at the hairpin. Sete tried to stick it out around the outside and the two rode side-by-side to the next turn, where they made contact – leaving Gibernau with a broken front fender. That unsettled the Spaniard, allowed Rossi to take victory by 0.456secs.

"I had a hard battle with Sete as I tried to overtake," said Rossi. *"At the next corner I almost lost the front and I thought I would crash. It was a fantastic race. I think Sete is a bit angry but it was a great race between us."*

Rossi's third victory in a row meant he and Gibernau were now tied at the top of the world championship standings, after six of 16 rounds.

04/07/2004

RIO GRAND PRIX

Rio could have been a disastrous race for Rossi, the Italian making a rare error and crashing out. However, Gibernau had already made a similar mistake and also failed to finish. *"What a shame. I lost the front and that was it,"* stated Rossi. *"I haven't fallen in a race since Mugello 2001. If I had managed to finish in fourth place it would have earned us some good points."*

25/07/2004

BRITISH
GRAND PRIX

With Rossi and Gibernau experiencing tough races in Rio and then Germany, Biaggi had been able to close to within one point of Rossi in the world championship. However, Rossi eased the pressure with a dominant performance at Donington Park and left the event 22 points ahead of Gibernau, while Biaggi dropped to third.

"I have taken a small advantage in the championship and at some tracks we will not have the advantage in race conditions so it is good to have these extra points," declared Rossi. *"I will sleep much better in the summer break."*

Rossi never put a wheel wrong, putting himself well clear at the top of the Championship.

05/09/2004

PORTUGUESE GRAND PRIX

Rossi's sixth win of the season came with a resounding five-second victory over Bridgestone-shod Honda rider Makoto Tamada at Estoril. Gibernau was only fourth, leaving him 29 points from Rossi, while Biaggi crashed out – effectively ending his title hopes. *"This was a super important race for us,"* said Rossi. *"I really wanted to push a lot from the beginning because I knew that if someone else was close at the end it would be really hard, because everyone's tyres would be moving around a lot."*

MALAYSIAN GRAND PRIX

Valle bounced back from his second non-finish of the season, at Qatar, with victory at Sepang – putting him on the brink of champion-ship victory. Rossi overcame the challenge of Honda riders Barros and Biaggi, while Gibernau was just seventh, handing Rossi a commanding 30-point lead heading into the final two rounds.

"It was very important for me to make a good result here, especially after Qatar," said Rossi, who celebrated by sweeping the track with a broom, a reference to Qatar, where he was forced to start from the back of the field after 'illegal' overnight grid-cleaning by his team. *"30 points is a good advantage but we need to concentrate because the championship lead was 39 points before Qatar, then much less after it. The battle is only over when it's over."*

"After Qatar, I said to Jerry Burgess we would go to Sepang and spank everybody's arse".

17/10/2004
AUSTRALIAN GRAND PRIX

Rossi's Yamaha dream became a reality at Phillip Island when the Italian won his sixth world championship and Yamaha's first since 1992 with a heart-stopping last lap victory over Gibernau.

Rossi was 0.2sec behind Gibernau as the final lap began and squeezed inside the #15 at turn two. Gibernau dived back underneath half a lap later, forcing Rossi to pull a breathtaking move as they accelerated over Lukey Heights. Rossi, who didn't even need to win the race to take the title, held on to victory by just 0.097sec!

After crossing the line a delighted Valentino hung over the front of his M1 to stroke his famous #46, before being mobbed by his waiting fan club – who gave him a t-shirt and helmet saying 'Che Spettacolo' ('The Show').

"Today was a fantastic finish to a fantastic championship," smiled Rossi. *"The last lap was a lot of fun for everybody watching it. I want to say thanks to everyone who has worked so hard, to Yamaha and all my team. It was fantastic, thank you. I think this has been my best championship."*

"This is like a dream come true for us all," said Rossi's team manager Davide Brivio. *"Like a movie with the best-ever storyline. If we wrote a script it could not have been better or more exciting."*

The 25-year-old had now taken four consecutive premier-class world championships and become the first rider since Eddie Lawson in 1989 to take back-to-back titles with different manufacturers.

31/10/2004

VALENCIA GRAND PRIX

Rossi won the 16th and final round of the 2004 season after battling bar-to-bar with the likes of Bayliss, Hayden, Tamada and finally Biaggi to take his ninth victory of the year by 0.4sec from the Roman.

"To win nine races is unbelievable and the finish of the season was perfect for us, three in a row. I had a tough fight with Tamada until he dropped back. Then there was a fight with Biaggi and he was also very strong. It is unbelievable to win here, and wonderful in front of this crowd. This year really has been unforgettable for me."

10/04/2005

SPANISH GRAND PRIX

The defining moment of the 2005 season came on the last corner of the very first round, when Rossi and Gibernau were fighting for victory at Jerez.

The pair had dominated the race, with Rossi taking the lead for the first time with three laps to go. Rossi then attempted to break away, but Gibernau met 'The Doctor's' challenge and was just a tenth of a second behind as the last lap began.

Gibernau reclaimed the lead when Rossi came close to crashing, then successfully rebuffed Rossi's counterattack leaving just one corner to go. It was now or never for Rossi and the determined Italian dived inside Gibernau under braking for the left hander.

The pair collided as their paths crossed at the apex – sending Gibernau off track, whilst Rossi rode to victory. Gibernau and the Spanish fans were outraged, but Rossi insisted it was hard but fair.

"Gibernau set a fast pace from the start but I just tried to stay with him and then attacked at the end," recalled Rossi. *"I got in front but I made a mistake on the last lap and Gibernau got past. We passed each other again but I got a better exit and there was enough space for me to pass him in the final corner, it was the only place where I could pass. We touched but motorbike races are sometimes like this. I know Sete is not happy but there are going to be 16 more races this year and there will be many more hard battles."*

2004

MOTOGP CHAMPION

01/05/2005

CHINESE GRAND PRIX

Having finished second to Barros in changeable weather at Estoril, Rossi won the first-ever Chinese motorcycle grand prix during monsoon conditions at Shanghai. Starting from sixth on the grid, Rossi took control on the fifth lap and survived late pressure from wild-card Olivier Jacque to win by 1.7sec.

"Out of all the victories in my career, this was the one I least expected – I am really surprised," said Rossi, now 13 points ahead of Gibernau's fast improving team-mate Marco Melandri in the world championship. *"It is the first time I have won in the wet on the Yamaha, so it is a special victory."*

15/05/2005

FRENCH GRAND PRIX

Gibernau returned to the front at Le Mans, but Rossi again had the upper hand – holding off his arch-rival by 0.38sec after a tense finale. Both riders recorded their fastest lap of the race on the last lap – but Rossi's was 0.2sec quicker.

"Gibernau arrived very fast so I decided to push to the maximum. Every lap I was better and better and I set the fastest time of the race on the final lap, so that shows the excellent progress we have made with the bike," said Rossi, who extended his world championship lead to 37 points over the consistent Melandri.

05/06/2005

ITALIAN GRAND PRIX

Rossi's home record reached four in a row with another victory at Mugello, this time by 0.36sec over Biaggi. Countrymen Capirossi and Melandri were third and fourth, while Gibernau crashed out.

"That was an incredible race and the best possible finish for the crowd, with four Italian riders in the top four positions. It was a great battle - full of passes," said Rossi, who wore a 'mortar board' on the podium, a reference to his recent honorary doctorate from an Italian university. *"I made my attack with three laps to go and it worked so of course I am very happy. It was an honour to race in front of this amazing crowd."*

On the 23rd lap, Rossi unleashed the inevitable. Taking a faster exit from the downhill corner onto the long front straight, he sped by on the inside and into turn one to set his blistering record lap, maintaining a similar pace to the finish.

GAULOISES   GAULOISES

12/06/2005

CATALAN GRAND PRIX

Rossi took a textbook victory over Gibernau in Barcelona; the world champion shadowing the home hero until three laps to go - when he coolly overtook, set a new lap record and went on to win his fifth race from the opening six rounds.

"I was a little worried before this weekend about the reaction from the crowd [after what happened at Jerez] but I was so happy with the reception I got. It shows that motorcycle fans are the best kind and especially here in Spain, where it is always a pleasure to ride," said Rossi, now 58 points in front of Melandri. *"The advantage in the championship is allowing the team to work in a relaxed way and we are having a lot of fun."*

25/06/2005
DUTCH TT

Rossi became the first Yamaha rider to win five consecutive 500cc/MotoGP races with victory in the 75th Dutch TT at Assen, the last event at the legendary circuit before much of its northern loop was removed. Rossi took his sixth victory from seven events by fighting forwards from fifth on lap one, then withstanding late race pressure from Melandri.

"Melandri was very strong and he came back to fight until the end," said Rossi, who won by 1.6sec. *"I can't believe I am the first Yamaha rider to win five races in a row, when you look at the company I am in with Yamaha's former world champions - Agostini, Lawson, Roberts and Rainey, it's great."*

History man Rossi took his sixth win of the year, and he became the first Yamaha rider to take five races in a row...

24/07/2005
BRITISH GRAND PRIX

Rossi's winning streak had ended at Laguna Seca, but the Italian floated back to the top during appalling conditions at Donington Park. Rossi initially lost ground from pole position, but recovered to leave Kenny Roberts Jr and Barros trailing in his 'wake'.

"Today was not like riding a bike, it was like riding a boat because there was a lot of water between the wheels and the track," said Rossi, before explaining his post-race celebration. *"Yesterday when I looked at my best lap time I thought it was like a symphony of violins - perfect, so I decided that if I won I would do this celebration across the finish line!"*

Rossi's championship advantage had now reached a massive 104 points over Melandri, with eight rounds still to go.

31/07/2005

GERMAN GRAND PRIX

> *"He reminds me of Mike Hailwood – not only with his talent, but in the fact that he puts lots of fun and enjoyment into his racing."*
> Phil Read

Rossi exploited a last lap error from Gibernau to narrowly beat four Honda riders at the Sachsenring, marking his eighth win from ten starts.

"Sete made a small mistake at the first braking marker, which is an easy thing to do when you are racing at this speed, and I was able to take the lead," explained Rossi. *"I don't know if I would have won if he hadn't made the mistake, but I would have tried!"*

The victory was Rossi's 76th in grand prix racing, moving him up to third in the all-time grand prix winners list alongside the late Mike Hailwood, whom Rossi honoured during his post-race celebrations.

"I made a special flag to apologise to Mike Hailwood for matching his 76 wins, because when another rider arrives at your level, it's always disappointing!" smiled Valentino. *"Mike is one of the greatest riders ever, and now I am beside him on the all-time winners 'podium' in grand prix, which is a fantastic achievement!"*

123

Gibernau, winless since 2004, suffered yet more bad luck at Brno when he ran out of fuel on the last lap at Brno, after a race long battle with Rossi.

"Gibernau was my hardest opponent so I tried to push him and put the pressure on from the start," revealed Rossi. *"It was a great fight with a lot of overtaking. Towards the end I made the pass on Sete and then did a perfect final lap. Unfortunately Sete had a problem, which was bad luck for him because he deserved to be on the podium. Anyway this is a good win for me and now I just need one more for the title, but it is not over yet."*

Rossi's title advantage now stood at 132 points over Melandri with six rounds (and 150 points) remaining.

JAPANESE GRAND PRIX

Rossi's warning that **"it is not over yet"** came to fruition next time out in Japan, when the Italian made a rare mistake and collided with Melandri, taking them both out of the race and leaving Marco with a nasty foot injury.

"It was the first time I had followed Marco into turn ten and we took completely different lines," Rossi explained. *"For the first 50m of braking we were at exactly the same speed so there was no warning, but he was able to stop the bike much harder than me and I couldn't avoid him. I wasn't even trying to pass him; it was just one of those things. I apologised to Marco and he said* 'it happens.' *Now I am very concerned for him and I just hope he is ok."*

25/09/2005
MALAYSIAN GRAND PRIX

Rossi won his fifth consecutive 500cc/MotoGP title by finishing second to Capirossi at Sepang, round 14 of 17. Rossi marked his seventh world title (in all classes) by wearing a t-shirt bearing the famous #7 worn by Barry Sheene, then joined his fan club for a special 'Snow White and the Seven Dwarfs' celebration!

"I am world champion for the seventh time, which is incredible!" smiled Rossi. *"Last year was a bit of a surprise but this time everybody was out to beat me."*

"I put the number 7 on my t-shirt because this is the number of my championships and also because it was the number of Barry Sheene, a great hero of mine," Rossi confirmed. *"The celebration with my fan club dressed as Snow White and the Seven Dwarfs was just a bit of fun to celebrate the seven titles. I always liked the story as a child!"*

01/10/2005

QATAR GRAND PRIX

Fresh from claiming his seventh world title, Rossi became the first Yamaha rider to win ten races in a single season during the *'best race of the year'* at Qatar. Long time leader Gibernau ran off track with five laps remaining, while Rossi repelled Melandri's final attack with just a few turns to go.

"What a race! For me that was the best of the season, it was so much fun," said Rossi. *"I had two great rivals, all three of us gave more than 100% and had a fantastic battle from the beginning to the end. Marco tried to pass me on the last lap but I was able to hold on and win - my tenth of the season. I am very, very happy."*

16/10/2005

AUSTRALIAN GRAND PRIX

Rossi equalled his 2002 Honda record of eleven wins in a season with his final victory of the 2005 season, in Australia. Rossi held off a strong challenge from Nicky Hayden to continue his undefeated run at Phillip Island, which began in 2001. The result meant that Yamaha added the 2005 constructors' championship to the already claimed riders' and teams' titles.

"It has been an amazing season and today we have won the constructors' title for Yamaha in the year of their 50th anniversary, so I am very happy," said Rossi. *"Congratulations to everybody. Eleven wins in the year matches my own record and to do it at Phillip Island is very special for me."*

Nothing could stop Rossi tying up the constructors' title for Yamaha. "Always to race in this track is different, is magic," he said. "I win a lot of times here, a lot of important races for my career. I love this track."

26/03/2006

SPANISH GRAND PRIX

The 2006 season began disastrously when Rossi – now riding in Camel colours – was knocked down by Toni Elias at turn one of the season-opening Spanish Grand Prix at Jerez. It was the kind of misfortune that would haunt Rossi's entire 2006 campaign.

"I saw Toni come up on the inside and he hit me; this is racing and these things happen. I have known Toni for many years and he is a good rider. He apologised to me after the race so I told him not to worry – only to remember to brake next time and if it is too late then to hit another bike instead of me!" joked Rossi, who remounted to finish 14th.

Rossi's bike problems would go on for some time yet, but his ability to maximise his strengths was devastating.

08/04/2006
QATAR GRAND PRIX

Rossi looked to get his 2006 season back on track with victory at round two in Qatar. The win – by 0.9sec over Hayden – was Rossi's 54th in 500cc/MotoGP and put him equal with Mick Doohan. Only the legendary Giacomo Agostini was now ahead of Rossi, with 68 victories.

"It is great to be level with Mick Doohan, now only Giacomo Agostini is ahead of me," confirmed Rossi. *"Records are not the most important thing but they are always nice! This feels like the start of the championship for me. Jerez was a nightmare but here we woke up!"*

However, Qatar was to prove a false dawn since it proved to be Rossi's only victory – and podium finish – during the first five rounds.

As usual, Rossi wore a special helmet for the event – by top Italian cartoonist Milo Manara, *"a mythical story of my life, with some of my heroes like Steve McQueen, Enzo Ferrari and Jim Morrison"*, plus Guido the bulldog and Osvaldo the Chicken.

04/06/2006

ITALIAN GRAND PRIX

ITALIAN GRAND PRIX

After just one fourth place finish from the previous three rounds, Rossi chances of a fifth consecutive home Mugello victory looked remote. But Valentino once again rose to the occasion, claiming a dramatic win over fellow Italian Capirossi, riding for Ducati, after a gladiatorial contest worthy of ancient Rome.

"That was one of the toughest battles of my entire career," acknowledged Rossi. *"Once Loris arrived I knew I was in for a hard fight. I decided to let him pass but I didn't realise so many other riders were so close and they all came through! Suddenly I was down in fifth and had it all to do again."*

"It was just an amazing fight for everybody and I think it is fantastic that it went down to the final lap between two riders, two factories, two tyre manufacturers but just one country! If I had to bet on who would win the last lap I honestly wouldn't have been able to choose. I don't think I took a breath over the last two laps but I made it and I am unbelievably happy."

Despite the victory, Rossi was only fifth in the world championship after six rounds, 34 points behind joint leaders Capirossi and Hayden.

Mugello belonged to Rossi, and Rossi belonged to Mugello. He gave the vast crowds exactly what they wanted.

ZZZ...

18/06/2006
CATALAN GRAND PRIX

Barcelona marked one of the few times in 2006 when Rossi was in a position to benefit from the misfortune of others. The Yamaha star claimed his second victory in a row by a comfortable 4.5sec from Hayden, but rivals Gibernau, Capirossi and Melandri were all absent after being injured during the initial race start.

"The restart was hard for everybody because we were all very worried about the riders who crashed - especially Marco because we could see his accident was a bad one," said Rossi. *"Just before the start Doctor Costa told me that Marco was more or less ok and I was very relieved. Even then it was tough to concentrate on re-starting the race."*

16/07/2006

GERMAN GRAND PRIX

Rossi's tough season had got even worse at round eight, Assen, when he was injured in practice. Rossi rode through the pain for valuable points at both Assen (eighth) and Donington Park (second), then delivered one of his greatest ever rides at the Sachsenring – where he won the closest top four finish in grand prix history, from just tenth on the grid!

Rossi took the lead for the first time on lap 13 (of 30) but couldn't shake-off the Hondas of Melandri, Hayden and Pedrosa. The Italian held on to a slim lead for all but one of the remaining laps, when Melandri made one of his many attacks stick, before crossing the line just 0.145sec ahead of Melandri, 0.266sec in front of Hayden and 0.307sec clear of fourth placed Pedrosa!

"That was an unbelievable race for me and my team," beamed Rossi, who climbed the podium with an Italian football shirt over his leathers, a reference to the national team's recent World Cup triumph. *"I had to battle with Dani, Nicky and Marco – each one was a great fight. Marco was so strong at the end of the race and I have to give my big congratulations to him, but thankfully I got the right line in the last corner and I was able to win. Italy became world champions in the football last weekend and I won today; Germany is a good country for us!"*

"Valentino is on another planet after what he has done today," said Herve Poncharal, boss of Yamaha's satellite MotoGP team.

10/09/2006

MALAYSIAN GRAND PRIX

After the high of his German GP win, Rossi came crashing down to earth when he suffered an engine failure at Laguna Seca, leaving him 51 points behind Hayden with six rounds to go.

Rossi began an epic fightback by finishing on the podium at each of the next five rounds, although his only victory during that time was at Sepang in Malaysia, when he emerged on top of a race long battle with Capirossi.

"That was another legendary battle between myself and Loris - very hard but also very fair," said Valentino. *"I enjoy racing with him so much because there is a lot of respect between us and a great trust – he is probably the hardest rival I have ever had but also one of my best friends in the paddock. For Pedrosa and Hayden to finish third and fourth is not ideal [for the championship] but all I can do is keep winning races."*

A sour note came later. Dani Pedrosa, grim-faced and pale, had a dogged and highly admirable ride to third. He had climbed out of a wheelchair onto his Honda after a heavy Friday crash. On the rostrum, Rossi appeared... with a chair. He sat in it, and took Capirossi in his lap, before they stood and sprayed champagne.

Suggestions were made that Valentino was making fun of his rival, but Rossi later denied any insult on Pedrosa. **"It is not in my character to make a joke about an injured rider,"** he insisted.

But there was one final twist in the tale – quite flabbergasting. What the packed stands – almost 130,000 people – saw was the most unexpected of all. Rossi off form. Rossi flustered. Rossi on the ground.

29/10/2006
VALENCIA
GRAND PRIX

Rossi's end-of-season charge, combined with a shocking mistake by Pedrosa at Estoril – when he collided with team-mate Hayden, taking them both out of the race – meant that Rossi arrived at the Valencian season finale holding an eight-point advantage over Hayden.

A sixth consecutive MotoGP title looked a mere formal-ity, especially after Rossi qualified on pole, but the Italian's dream run of title success came to an end when a nervous start was followed by a mistake on lap five, when he lost the front of his Yamaha while holding seventh position. Rossi remounted to finish 13th, but third place for Hayden gave him the title.

"Of course this is a big disappointment for me because to arrive at the final race with an eight-point advantage and then not win the title is a disaster," confessed Rossi. *"Basically I made two mistakes today – one was at the start and then the second one was the crash. It has been a very emotional season, with some great moments, some bad luck and now some mistakes. But this is racing. All I can say now is a big 'congratulations' to Nicky because he is a great guy, a great rider and he is the world champion because he has been the best this year."*

25/03/2007

SPANISH GRAND PRIX

After the shock of Casey Stoner's debut victory in the Qatar season opener, Rossi looked to restore order with an uncompromising victory over Pedrosa at round two in Jerez. Rossi marked his return to the top step of the podium with a game of human skittles on the side of the track!

"It feels like a long time since I last won and this is a great emotion and a very special victory for me," said Rossi, now riding in Fiat colours. *"I got a great start, didn't make any mistakes and had a good battle with Pedrosa, who we knew would be the danger today. Now we have two race tracks which might be difficult for us so it's very important to leave here leading the championship."*

2007

An important victory. "The faster upcoming tracks would not offer such opportunities." Prophetic words indeed.

03/06/2007

ITALIAN GRAND PRIX

The optimism created by Rossi's Jerez victory soon drifted away as it became clear that Yamaha's (Michelin-shod) first 800cc MotoGP machine was no match for Stoner's powerful Bridgestone-shod Ducati Desmosedici.

Rossi finished behind Stoner in the four rounds leading up to his home Italian Grand Prix, but once again defied the odds to increase his run of Mugello victories to a record six in a row.

Riding with a red heart on his helmet, Rossi was forced to dig deep as he slumped from the front row to eighth, but kept his cool and began scything through the field. Rossi took the lead from Pedrosa on lap nine of 23 and edged three seconds clear of the Spaniard by the finish.

"It was really a perfect race and I felt like I had everyone on my side; Mugello is a magical track for me and this victory gives us a lot of power and confidence for the next races," said Rossi. *"I had a special helmet for this race with a big heart on it and today I think we showed that we really have a lot of heart at Yamaha. This is a great, great moment for me."*

Towering genius is Rossi's trademark, and that is what drove the capacity crowd into frenzies of delight with his sixth straight win at the magnificent Mugello circuit.

Mugello 2007

30/06/2007
DUTCH TT

Rossi won a straight fight with Stoner for the first time in the 2007 season at Assen - when the Italian charged from eleventh on the grid to pass the young Australian with four laps to go.

Riding in a special 'retro' Fiat 500 livery, Rossi passed rider after rider to reach second position behind Stoner by lap 12 of 26. Rossi remained locked to Stoner's rear wheel, before launching a carefully planned attack at the chicane with three laps to go – then bolting to his third victory of the season and Yamaha's 150th in 500cc/MotoGP.

30/06/2007
DUTCH TT

"This was an incredible race. I think maybe one of the top five of my career!" said Rossi. *"Last night I didn't sleep so well and I couldn't have imagined that the race could turn out like this."*

"Once I got going though I saw that I had a great pace and so I just rode as hard as I could to get past everyone because I knew then that I could come back to Casey. When I finally got there I was quite tired, as were my tyres, plus he was riding very well and it was hard to overtake him, but my M1 worked brilliantly today and in the last few laps I was able to go past and win."

"I'm so happy to win here in Assen, it's a special place for me and this is a great emotion! It was nice to have a special livery here as well, in the past I haven't been so lucky with new liveries but hopefully today has turned that around! Congratulations to Yamaha for 150 wins, I am glad that we could celebrate like this!"

15/07/2007
GERMAN GRAND PRIX

Rossi left Assen 21 points behind Stoner, but this accident next time out at the Sachsenring put Stoner's advantage back up to 32 points.

Rossi started from sixth but dropped to eighth and was forced to push hard to try and get back in touch with the leaders. Rossi's haste caught him out on lap six, when he fell just moments after over-taking Randy de Puniet for sixth.

"Unfortunately I made a mistake today and I want to say sorry to everyone," said Rossi. *"Getting past de Puniet was hard because in the part of the track where it's best to overtake he was very fast. Finally I made my move and I made a great pass but I made a mistake and lost the front."*

Sachsenring marked a rare occasion when Stoner's Bridgestone tyres struggled, but Rossi was unable to exploit the situation. *"I'm so disappointed because our package was working very well and we missed the chance to make up a lot of points on Stoner."* [who finished fifth] admitted Rossi.

Rossi just leaned it over too far. He went down, with de Puniet looking over his shoulder in astonishment. And that was it. With bent levers, his bike was too damaged to ride. He left the track on foot, his head cast down.

Rossi's fourth and final victory of 2007 came at Estoril, when the Italian won his first race since June by edging out a determined Pedrosa by just 0.175sec. After three start-to-finish wins by Stoner, the race also marked a welcome return to close racing.

"I want to dedicate this victory to Colin McRae, who sadly died yesterday. Colin is one of my idols and it's because of him that I have my passion for rally," began Rossi. *"I am glad that I could win for him today and it's a great emotion to win again after four races without even a podium. I had a great battle with Casey but most of all with Dani and it was fantastic fun to ride like this again, at the maximum and with a lot of good passes."*

Despite Rossi's victory, third place for Stoner put him on the brink of the world title, which he secured next time out in Japan. Rossi meanwhile slumped to third in the championship, his worst ranking since his 1996 125cc debut, with just one podium from the last four races.

159

2008

04/05/2008

CHINESE GRAND PRIX

Rossi's return to reclaim his crown was a great achievement, because the competition was fiercer than any he had faced in his career...

GRAND PRIX OF CHINA
Shanghai 2008

Rossi's first win of the 2008 season – and first-ever with Bridgestone tyres – came at round four, the Chinese Grand Prix at Shanghai. Rossi earned victory after a tense battle with Pedrosa, whose challenge Rossi finally broke with three laps to go. The victory marked the end of Rossi's longest losing streak since 2000.

"After seven races it is a great feeling to win again; I am very happy!" said Rossi. *"I had a great battle with Pedrosa and he pushed me hard. It's the first win with Bridgestone so this is a great moment. We've had four races and four different winners so this shows how close the championship is, now we need to keep going because our rivals are all very near."*

Rossi left Shanghai third in the world championship, two points behind rookie team-mate Jorge Lorenzo and nine points from Pedrosa.

FRENCH GRAND PRIX

Immediately after his first win of the season, Rossi became the first double winner of the year with a comprehensive five-second victory over Lorenzo at Le Mans.

The win was Rossi's 90th in grand prix racing, placing him alongside Angel Nieto as the second most successful rider of all time. The Spanish legend of the '60s, '70s and '80s, who won 13 world titles in the smaller grand prix classes, played a central part in Rossi's post-race celebrations by riding Valentino's bike with him on the slow down lap.

"To arrive at 90 wins and equal Angel's record is a dream for me," said Rossi. *"I had quite a lot of pressure because Angel was waiting with the special leathers to join me on the bike, so I really needed to win! It was great to ride with him. 180 victories together on one bike is quite impressive I think!"*

Fourth for Pedrosa meant Rossi also took the world championship lead for the first time.

A respecter of the past, Rossi's acknowledgment of Nieto was very proper...

Rossi the showman aways does something special for his home GP at Mugello, and his latest helmet design was the most extraordinary to date.

Rossi's face depicted in mock terror was on the top of his helmet making for and extraordinary sight as the Yamaha rider braked from 200mph at the end of the main straight. *"I think it's the best yet,"* said Rossi.

01/06/2008

ITALIAN GRAND PRIX

Rossi's incredible Mugello form continued in 2008 when the home star notched up his seventh consecutive victory. Riding with a special helmet design – featuring a picture of his face on the top! – Rossi took the lead on lap four and remained out of reach for the rest of the race.

Valentino is pictured above with two of motorcycle racing's legends Angel Nieto and Giacomo Agostini.

01/06/2008

ITALIAN GRAND PRIX

"After winning the championship, winning at Mugello is the next best thing for me and once again today it was like a dream," said Rossi. *"There is no way to describe the feeling I have standing on the podium in front of all of my fans here and I am so happy that I could win once again today. To win for the seventh time running at my home track is amazing but I felt quite a lot of pressure about this, so it's a relief as well because I didn't want to disappoint everyone!"*

Rossi's title lead now stood at twelve points over Pedrosa.

08/06/2008
CATALAN GRAND PRIX

Pedrosa proved untouchable in front of his home fans at Catalunya, his second victory of the year on Spanish asphalt, but Rossi – who qualified just ninth – was at least able to limit the damage by winning a tough fight for second against Stoner.

"It's a long time since we've had a good fight for the top positions like that and today it was like last year with Stoner, but for second instead of first place!" said Rossi. *"Pedrosa was incredibly strong today and I think it's impossible to say whether or not I could have gone with him even if I had started from the front."*

Rossi was riding in a special Italian football team livery, to mark the start of the European Football Championships.

VALENTINO ROSSI

DUTCH TT

UNITED STATES GRAND PRIX

Rossi's only race mistake during the 2008 season came on lap one of the Dutch TT. Rossi had made a slow start from third on the grid, then lost the back of his M1 on the entry to a tight left hand hairpin – the rear wheel whipping around and swiping Randy de Puniet from his LCR Honda.

"After seven podiums in a row I made a mistake today – this is racing!" said Rossi. *"I arrived too fast when the tyres were still cold, I was too hard on the brakes and I lost the rear. I am sincerely sorry to Randy de Puniet and all of his team."*

Rossi was able to rejoin a distant last and finished the race in eleventh, costing him the world championship lead to Pedrosa, with Assen winner Stoner now just 25 points from Rossi in third.

The showdown between Rossi and Stoner reinforced the former's reputation as one of the greatest of all time...

The turning point of the 2008 season came at Laguna Seca, when Rossi defied the odds to inflict a stunning victory over man-of-the-moment Stoner. The Australian had dominated the previous three rounds and qualified on pole for the US GP by almost half a second from Rossi.

But when the red lights went out Rossi launched a relentless barrage against the Australian – retaliating whenever Stoner took the lead to prevent the #1 using his superior speed to disappear into the distance.

Casey's frustration eventually got the better of him and he ran off track with eight laps to go, allowing Rossi to cruise to his fourth victory of the year and deliver a major psychological blow to Stoner. Stoner initially refused to shake Rossi's hand after the race, but had calmed down a little by the podium ceremony.

"What a race!" said Rossi. *"We made some modifications to our bike and that enabled me to fight with Casey today. I knew I had to try and stay in front of him and it was impossible to relax even for one second. Casey was a bit faster on the straight but I was stronger on the brakes. I don't know how many times we changed the lead but it was a lot and it was great, great racing. I am sorry that Casey thinks some of the passes were a bit strong but I really don't agree; I passed only on the brakes, I braked in the same places every time and we never touched. Of course this was an aggressive race, but it was definitely a fair one."*

Above: An ecstatic Valentino embraces his Fiat Yamaha crew after taking his fifth win of the season.

Right: With his chief rivals Stoner and Pedrosa out of the points, Rossi shares the podium with Toni Elias and Loris Capirossi.

Below: Five time champion in the senior class, Mick Doohan shares a joke with Valentino who would soon go on to overtake the Australian's total in taking a sixth win.

17/08/2008

CZECH REPUBLIC GRAND PRIX

Rossi's grip on the 2008 world championship tightened when his title advantage over Stoner doubled to 50 points next time out at Brno. Rossi was closing on Stoner when the Australian fell from the lead, gifting Rossi victory.

"Casey was incredibly fast at the start but after two laps I understood that my bike was working very well and that I was fast enough to try to catch him. I closed a little and gradually the red bike was becoming a bit bigger in front of me. I think this is when he started to push harder and made his mistake. I was anticipating a very hard battle if I did catch him, so when I saw the red bike slide out I could hardly believe it – this made things a lot easier for me!"

SAN MARINO GRAND PRIX

Rossi matched countryman Giacomo Agostini's all-time record of 68 premier-class victories with an emotional victory at his 'local' Misano circuit, after Stoner fell from the lead for the second race in succession.

"Today is a truly fantastic day and I can't believe that I have matched Agostini's record! He was one of my heroes so it's quite incredible to have made it to 68 wins," said Rossi. *"Mugello has always been 'my' track, even though it's further away from Tavullia, but here we haven't found it so easy."*

"Once I was past Dani I could see Casey, although I have to admit that I wasn't as confident as I was in Brno that I could win. Anyway I kept pushing and I think it still could have been a battle. Then I saw Casey slide out. I'm sorry for him once again but this is very good for our championship."

Rossi's third win in a row meant he was now 75 points clear of Stoner, with five rounds left and a maximum 125 points to be won.

Rossi's victory at Misano put him equal on premier-class wins with Giacomo Agostini — on 68.

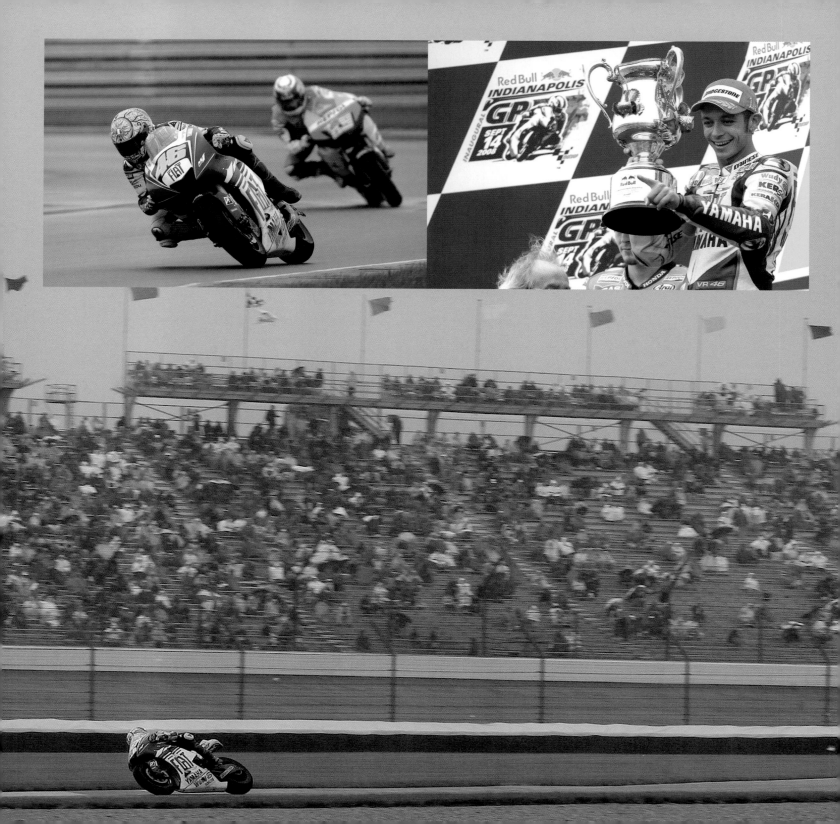

Right: Rossi and his crew celebrate the rider's record-breaking 69th premier-class victory.

Left: It seemed fitting that Valentino would be the rider to post the first MotoGP victory at the historic Indianapolis Motor Speedway.

Far left: Local hero Nicky Hayden gave of his best in the weather conditions, but could not match Ross's pace.

14/09/2008

INDIANAPOLIS GRAND PRIX

Rossi's 69th premier-class victory came during MotoGP's storm-shortened debut at Indianapolis Motor Speedway. Rossi overcome local star Hayden and some appalling weather conditions before the red flags were finally shown with seven of the 28 laps to go, confirming Rossi's seventh victory of the season and fourth in a row.

"This is fantastic because it's been a long time since I won in the rain and even longer since I won four in a row!" said Rossi, now on the brink of clinching the 2008 world title. *"To win the first race here at Indianapolis is a great emotion and to beat Agostini's record is also incredible, now I hope my record will stand for 30 years like his!"*

28/09/2008
JAPANESE GRAND PRIX

Rossi became only the second rider in history (alongside Agostini) to recapture the premier-class title after two successive defeats by wrapping up the 2008 world championship in perfect style, with victory in Yamaha's home race at Motegi.

The 29-year-old battled title rivals Stoner and Pedrosa for the first half of the event, but was untouchable thereafter and claimed his eighth victory of the year by nearly two seconds from Stoner.

Rossi was now a six-time MotoGP world champion – a statistic bettered only by Agostini – and an eight-time title winner in all three grand prix classes.

"It's a great victory and a great achievement; I think it's at the same level as the first title in 2004 with Yamaha, maybe even better!" said Rossi. *"It was a fantastic feeling to take the title with a win, like I did in 2001 and 2004. I think this is the hardest I have ever had to work to win a world championship and I have to say a huge thank you to everyone involved for working this hard alongside me."*

"I also have to say a special thank you to Bridgestone, they have done a great job with the tyres and the decision to be with them has been a big part of our success this season".

"We have lost for two years and I don't think I was the favourite this season, but we have shown that we are a great team and that we never give up," added Rossi, who celebrated with a t-shirt saying *'sorry for the delay'*. *"I am so happy that I have now won three titles with Yamaha because this is how many I won with [Honda]. I hope we will have more together! Now I have to get used to being world champion again!"*

"When you try to finish second things can go wrong."
Rossi put the championship to bed with his eighth win of the year at Motegi.

MALAYSIAN GRAND PRIX

Rossi's ninth and final victory of 2008 came at the penultimate round, when The Doctor took a cool and calculating victory at a scorching hot Sepang circuit. Rossi studied Pedrosa until the midway point of the race, when he made his victory pass and escaped.

"I am so happy with this win today because in all of the toughest championship of my career, including with Yamaha in 2004, I have taken nine victories," said Rossi, whose bike had a special sticker to mark the passing of his pet bulldog. *"Today was incredibly hard because it was so hot. Lap-by-lap I understood better where it was possible to overtake Dani and eventually I could make my move and go away from him."*

Rossi won with a clinical display of dominance in the punishing heat...

03/05/2009

SPANISH GRAND PRIX

2009

Having been forced to play second-fiddle to Casey Stoner in Qatar and then Yamaha team mate Jorge Lorenzo in Japan, Valentino bounced back emphatically to claim victory at the Spanish Grand Prix in Jerez. The portents for the race were not good, with Rossi having managed only fourth place on the grid after a difficult time in qualifying. But a major change in set-up on the Italian's Yamaha M1 by Jerry Burgess and his crew overnight put the Italian back on the pace.

Starting fourth, it took just two laps for Valentino to displace his team mate Lorenzo and then set off in pursuit of Casey Stoner and the leader Dani Pedrosa. Valentino caught and passed the Australian rider, who retaliated immediately, but by the end of lap seven Rossi finally overcame the Ducati rider's resistance and set off in pursuit of the leader. For a while it was stalemate between the pair, but at two-thirds distance Valentino began to gradually haul in the plucky Honda rider before making a decisive move with ten laps remaining. From then on Rossi controlled proceedings to record his 98th Grand Prix career victory in all classes.

SPANISH GRAND PRIX

"I hope that the changes we've made here will help us for the rest of the season. Thanks again to everyone!"

VALENTINO ROSSI
GRAND PRIX CAREER RECORD

1996-2009

Pos	Event	Circuit	No.	Entrant	Machine	Comment
1996						
	125cc; Championship position: 9th, Wins: 1, Poles: 1, Fastest laps: 2, Points: 111					
6	MALAYSIAN GP	Shah Alam	46	Team Polini	Aprilia RS125	
11	INDONESIAN GP	Sentul	46	Team Polini	Aprilia RS125	
11	JAPANESE GP	Suzuka	46	Team Polini	Aprilia RS125	
4	SPANISH GP	Jerez	46	Team Polini	Aprilia RS125	
4	ITALIAN GP	Mugello	46	Team Polini	Aprilia RS125	
ret	FRENCH GP	Paul Ricard	46	Team Polini	Aprilia RS125	crashed out - lap 24; F.Lap
ret	DUTCH GP	Assen	46	Team Polini	Aprilia RS125	crashed out - lap 8
5	GERMAN GP	Nürburgring	46	Team Polini	Aprilia RS125	
ret	BRITISH GP	Donington	46	Team Polini	Aprilia RS125	mechanical
3	AUSTRIAN GP	A-1 Ring	46	Team Polini	Aprilia RS125	
1	CZECH GP	Brno	46	Team Polini	Aprilia RS125	Pole
5	IMOLA GP	Imola	46	Team Polini	Aprilia RS125	F.Lap
ret	CATALUNYA GP	Barcelona	46	Team Polini	Aprilia RS125	multiple crash - lap 1
ret	RIO GP	Rio de Janeiro	46	Team Polini	Aprilia RS125	crashed out - lap 1
14	AUSTRALIAN GP	Eastern Creek	46	Team Polini	Aprilia RS125	
1997						
	125cc: CHAMPION, Wins: 11, Poles: 4, Fastest laps: 7, Points: 321					
1	MALAYSIAN GP	Shah Alam	46	Nastro Azzurro Aprilia	Aprilia RS125	Pole; F.Lap
ret	JAPANESE GP	Suzuka	46	Nastro Azzurro Aprilia	Aprilia RS125	crashed out - lap 16
1	SPANISH GP	Jerez	46	Nastro Azzurro Aprilia	Aprilia RS125	F.Lap
1	ITALIAN GP	Mugello	46	Nastro Azzurro Aprilia	Aprilia RS125	
2	AUSTRIAN GP	A-1 Ring	46	Nastro Azzurro Aprilia	Aprilia RS125	F.Lap
1	FRENCH GP	Paul Ricard	46	Nastro Azzurro Aprilia	Aprilia RS125	
1	DUTCH TT	Assen	46	Nastro Azzurro Aprilia	Aprilia RS125	Pole
1	IMOLA GP	Imola	46	Nastro Azzurro Aprilia	Aprilia RS125	Pole; F.Lap
1	GERMAN GP	Nürburgring	46	Nastro Azzurro Aprilia	Aprilia RS125	Pole
1	RIO GP	Rio de Janeiro	46	Nastro Azzurro Aprilia	Aprilia RS125	F.Lap
1	BRITISH GP	Donington	46	Nastro Azzurro Aprilia	Aprilia RS125	F.Lap
3	CZECH GP	Brno	46	Nastro Azzurro Aprilia	Aprilia RS125	
1	CATALUNYA GP	Barcelona	46	Nastro Azzurro Aprilia	Aprilia RS125	
1	INDONESIAN GP	Sentul	46	Nastro Azzurro Aprilia	Aprilia RS125	F.Lap
6	AUSTRALIAN GP	Phillip Island	46	Nastro Azzurro Aprilia	Aprilia RS125	

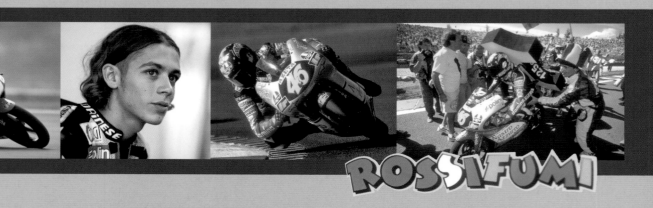

ROSSIFUMI

1998

250cc; Championship position: 2nd, Wins: 5, Poles: 0, Fastest laps: 3, Points: 201

ret	JAPANESE GP	Suzuka	46	Team Aprilia Racing	Aprilia RS250	engine - 10 laps
ret	MALAYSIAN GP	Johor Circuit	46	Team Aprilia Racing	Aprilia RS250	crashed out - lap 27; F.Lap
2	SPANISH GP	Jerez	46	Team Aprilia Racing	Aprilia RS250	
2	ITALIAN GP	Mugello	46	Team Aprilia Racing	Aprilia RS250	
2	FRENCH GP	Paul Ricard	46	Team Aprilia Racing	Aprilia RS250	
ret	MADRID GP	Jarama	46	Team Aprilia Racing	Aprilia RS250	crash damage - lap 4
1	DUTCH TT	Assen	46	Team Aprilia Racing	Aprilia RS250	
ret	BRITISH GP	Donington	46	Team Aprilia Racing	Aprilia RS250	crashed out - lap 2
3	GERMAN GP	Sachsenring	46	Team Aprilia Racing	Aprilia RS250	
ret	CZECH GP	Brno	46	Team Aprilia Racing	Aprilia RS250	crashed out - lap 1
1	IMOLA GP	Imola	46	Team Aprilia Racing	Aprilia RS250	
1	CATALAN GP	Barcelona	46	Team Aprilia Racing	Aprilia RS250	F.Lap
1	AUSTRALIAN GP	Phillip Island	46	Team Aprilia Racing	Aprilia RS250	
1	ARGENTINE GP	Buenos Aires	46	Team Aprilia Racing	Aprilia RS250	F.Lap

1999

250cc: CHAMPION, Wins: 9, Poles: 2, Fastest laps: 10, Points: 309

5	MALAYSIAN GP	Sepang	46	Team Aprilia Racing	Aprilia RS250	F.Lap
7	JAPANESE GP	Motegi	46	Team Aprilia Racing	Aprilia RS250	
1	SPANISH GP	Jerez	46	Team Aprilia Racing	Aprilia RS250	
ret	FRENCH GP	Paul Ricard	46	Team Aprilia Racing	Aprilia RS250	broken chain - lap 28; Pole; F.Lap
1	ITALIAN GP	Mugello	46	Team Aprilia Racing	Aprilia RS250	F.Lap
1	CATALAN GP	Barcelona	46	Team Aprilia Racing	Aprilia RS250	F.Lap
2	DUTCH TT	Assen	46	Team Aprilia Racing	Aprilia RS250	Pole; F.Lap
1	BRITISH GP	Donington	46	Team Aprilia Racing	Aprilia RS250	
1	GERMAN GP	Sachsenring	46	Team Aprilia Racing	Aprilia RS250	F.Lap
1	CZECH GP	Brno	46	Team Aprilia Racing	Aprilia RS250	F.Lap
2	IMOLA GP	Imola	46	Team Aprilia Racing	Aprilia RS250	
8	VALENCIA GP	Valencia	46	Team Aprilia Racing	Aprilia RS250	
1	AUSTRALIAN GP	Phillip Island	46	Team Aprilia Racing	Aprilia RS250	F.Lap
1	S. AFRICAN GP	Phakisa Circuit	46	Team Aprilia Racing	Aprilia RS250	F.Lap
1	RIO GP	Rio de Janeiro	46	Team Aprilia Racing	Aprilia RS250	F.Lap
3	ARGENTINE GP	Buenos Aires	46	Team Aprilia Racing	Aprilia RS250	

2000

500cc; Championship position: 2nd, Wins: 2, Poles: 0, Fastest laps: 5, Points: 209

ret	AFRICA'S GP	Phasika Circuit	46	Team Nastro Azzurro Honda	Honda NSR500	crashed out - lap 12; F.Lap
ret	MALAYSIAN GP	Sepang	46	Team Nastro Azzurro Honda	Honda NSR500	crashed out - lap 4
11	JAPANESE GP	Suzuka	46	Team Nastro Azzurro Honda	Honda NSR500	
3*	SPANISH GP	Jerez	46	Team Nastro Azzurro Honda	Honda NSR500	*Aggregate of 2 parts
3	FRENCH GP	Le Mans	46	Team Nastro Azzurro Honda	Honda NSR500	F.Lap
12	ITALIAN GP	Mugello	46	Team Nastro Azzurro Honda	Honda NSR500	
3	CATALAN GP	Barcelona	46	Team Nastro Azzurro Honda	Honda NSR500	
6	DUTCH TT	Assen	46	Team Nastro Azzurro Honda	Honda NSR500	
1	BRITISH GP	Donington	46	Team Nastro Azzurro Honda	Honda NSR500	
2	GERMAN GP	Sachsenring	46	Team Nastro Azzurro Honda	Honda NSR500	
2	CZECH GP	Brno	46	Team Nastro Azzurro Honda	Honda NSR500	
3	PORTUGUESE GP	Estoril	46	Team Nastro Azzurro Honda	Honda NSR500	F.Lap
ret	VALENCIA GP	Valencia	46	Team Nastro Azzurro Honda	Honda NSR500	crashed out - lap 26
1	BRAZILAN GP	Rio de Janeiro	46	Team Nastro Azzurro Honda	Honda NSR500	F.Lap
2	PACIFIC GP	Motegi	46	Team Nastro Azzurro Honda	Honda NSR500	F.Lap
3	AUSTRALIAN GP	Phillip Island	46	Team Nastro Azzurro Honda	Honda NSR500	

2001

500cc: CHAMPION, Wins: 11, Poles: 5, Fastest laps: 11, Points: 325

1	JAPANESE GP	Suzuka	46	Team Nastro Azzurro Honda	Honda NSR 500	
1	AFRICA'S GP	Phasika Circuit	46	Team Nastro Azzurro Honda	Honda NSR 500	Pole; F.Lap
1	SPANISH GP	Jerez	46	Team Nastro Azzurro Honda	Honda NSR 500	Pole; F.Lap
3	FRENCH GP	Le Mans	46	Team Nastro Azzurro Honda	Honda NSR 500	F.Lap
ret	ITALIAN GP	Mugello	46	Team Nastro Azzurro Honda	Honda NSR 500	crashed out - lap 22; Pole; F.Lap
1	CATALAN GP	Barcelona	46	Team Nastro Azzurro Honda	Honda NSR 500	Pole; F.Lap
2	DUTCH TT	Assen	46	Team Nastro Azzurro Honda	Honda NSR 500	F.Lap
1	BRITISH GP	Donington	46	Team Nastro Azzurro Honda	Honda NSR 500	Pole; F.Lap
7	GERMAN GP	Sachsenring	46	Team Nastro Azzurro Honda	Honda NSR 500	
1	CZECH GP	Brno	46	Team Nastro Azzurro Honda	Honda NSR 500	F.Lap
1	PORTUGUESE GP	Estoril	46	Team Nastro Azzurro Honda	Honda NSR 500	
11	VALENCIA GP	Valencia	46	Team Nastro Azzurro Honda	Honda NSR 500	wrong tyre choice
1	PACIFIC GP	Motegi	46	Team Nastro Azzurro Honda	Honda NSR 500	F.Lap
1	AUSTRALIAN GP	Phillip Island	46	Team Nastro Azzurro Honda	Honda NSR 500	
1	MALAYSIAN GP	Sepang	46	Team Nastro Azzurro Honda	Honda NSR 500	F.Lap
1	RIO GP	Rio de Janeiro	46	Team Nastro Azzurro Honda	Honda NSR 500	F.Lap

2002

MotoGP: CHAMPION, Wins: 11, Poles: 6, Fastest laps: 10, Points: 355

1	JAPANESE GP	Suzuka	46	Repsol Honda Team	Honda RCV 211 V5	Pole; F.Lap
2	AFRICA'S GP	Phakisa Circuit	46	Repsol Honda Team	Honda RCV 211 V5	Pole
1	SPANISH GP	Jerez	46	Repsol Honda Team	Honda RCV 211 V5	Pole; F.Lap
1	FRENCH GP	Le Mans	46	Repsol Honda Team	Honda RCV 211 V5	Pole; F.Lap
1	ITALIAN GP	Mugello	46	Repsol Honda Team	Honda RCV 211 V5	F.Lap
1	CATALAN GP	Barcelona	46	Repsol Honda Team	Honda RCV 211 V5	F.Lap
1	DUTCH TT	Assen	46	Repsol Honda Team	Honda RCV 211 V5	Pole; F.Lap
1	BRITISH GP	Donington	46	Repsol Honda Team	Honda RCV 211 V5	Pole; F.Lap
1	GERMAN GP	Sachsenring	46	Repsol Honda Team	Honda RCV 211 V5	F.Lap
ret	CZECH GP	Brno	46	Repsol Honda Team	Honda RCV 211 V5	tyre failure
1	PORTUGUESE GP	Estoril	46	Repsol Honda Team	Honda RCV 211 V5	F.Lap
1	RIO GP	Rio de Janeiro	46	Repsol Honda Team	Honda RCV 211 V5	
2	PACIFIC GP	Motegi	46	Repsol Honda Team	Honda RCV 211 V5	
2	MALAYSIAN GP	Sepang	46	Repsol Honda Team	Honda RCV 211 V5	
1	AUSTRALIAN GP	Phillip Island	46	Repsol Honda Team	Honda RCV 211 V5	F.Lap
2	VALENCIA GP	Valencia	46	Repsol Honda Team	Honda RCV 211 V5	

2003

MotoGP: CHAMPION, Wins: 9, Poles: 9, Fastest laps: 12, Points: 357

1	JAPANESE GP	Suzuki	46	Repsol Honda Team	Honda RC211 V5	Pole; F.Lap
2	AFRICA'S GP	Phakisa Circuit	46	Repsol Honda Team	Honda RC211 V5	F.Lap
1	SPANISH GP	Jerez	46	Repsol Honda Team	Honda RC211 V5	F.Lap
2	FRENCH GP	Le Mans	46	Repsol Honda Team	Honda RC211 V5	Pole
1	ITALIAN GP	Mugello	46	Repsol Honda Team	Honda RC211 V5	Pole
2	CATALAN GP	Barcelona	46	Repsol Honda Team	Honda RC211 V5	Pole; F.Lap
3	DUTCH TT	Assen	46	Repsol Honda Team	Honda RC211 V5	
3	BRITISH GP	Donington	46	Repsol Honda Team	Honda RC211 V5	F.Lap
2	GERMAN GP	Sachsenring	46	Repsol Honda Team	Honda RC211 V5	
1	CZECH GP	Brno	46	Repsol Honda Team	Honda RC211 V5	Pole; F.Lap
1	PORTUGUESE GP	Estoril	46	Repsol Honda Team	Honda RC211 V5	F.Lap
1	BRAZILIAN GP	Rio de Janeiro	46	Repsol Honda Team	Honda RC211 V5	Pole; F.Lap
2	PACIFIC GP	Motegi	46	Repsol Honda Team	Honda RC211 V5	F.Lap
1	MALAYSIAN GP	Sepang	46	Repsol Honda Team	Honda RC211 V5	Pole; F.Lap
1	AUSTRALIAN GP	Phillip Island	46	Repsol Honda Team	Honda RC211 V5	Pole; F.Lap
1	VALENCIA GP	Valencia	46	Repsol Honda Team	Honda RC211 V5	Pole; F.Lap

VALENTINIK

2004

MotoGP: CHAMPION, Wins: 9, Poles: 5, Fastest laps: 3, Points: 304

1	AFRICA'S GP	Phkisa Circuit	46	Gauloises Fortuna Yamaha Team	Yamaha M1	Pole
4	SPANISH GP	Jerez	46	Gauloises Fortuna Yamaha Team	Yamaha M1	Pole
4	FRENCH GP	Le Mans	46	Gauloises Fortuna Yamaha Team	Yamaha M1	
1*	ITALIAN GP	Mugello	46	Gauloises Fortuna Yamaha Team	Yamaha M1	*Restarted race, 6 laps
1	CATALAN GP	Barcelona	46	Gauloises Fortuna Yamaha Team	Yamaha M1	
1	DUTCH TT	Assen	46	Gauloises Fortuna Yamaha Team	Yamaha M1	Pole; F.Lap
ret	RIO GP	Rio de Janeiro	46	Gauloises Fortuna Yamaha Team	Yamaha M1	crashed out - lap 12
4	GERMAN GP	Sachsenring	46	Gauloises Fortuna Yamaha Team	Yamaha M1	
1	BRITISH GP	Donington	46	Gauloises Fortuna Yamaha Team	Yamaha M1	Pole
2	CZECH GP	Brno	46	Gauloises Fortuna Yamaha Team	Yamaha M1	
1	PORTUGUESE GP	Estoril	46	Gauloises Fortuna Yamaha Team	Yamaha M1	F.Lap
2	JAPANESE GP	Motegi	46	Gauloises Fortuna Yamaha Team	Yamaha M1	
ret	QATAR GP	Losail Citcuit	46	Gauloises Fortuna Yamaha Team	Yamaha M1	
1	MALAYSIAN GP	Sepang	46	Gauloises Fortuna Yamaha Team	Yamaha M1	Pole; F.Lap
1	AUSTRALIAN GP	Phillip Island	46	Gauloises Fortuna Yamaha Team	Yamaha M1	
1	VALENCIA GP	Valencia	46	Gauloises Fortuna Yamaha Team	Yamaha M1	

2005

MotoGP: CHAMPION, Wins: 11, Poles: 5, Fastest laps: 6, Points: 367

1	SPANISH GP	Jerez	46	Gauloises Yamaha Team	Yamaha M1	Pole; F.Lap
2	PORTUGUESE GP	Estoril	46	Gauloises Yamaha Team	Yamaha M1	
1	CHINESE GP	Shanghai	46	Gauloises Yamaha Team	Yamaha M1	
1	FRENCH GP	Le Mans	46	Gauloises Yamaha Team	Yamaha M1	Pole; F.Lap
1	ITALIAN GP	Mugello	46	Gauloises Yamaha Team	Yamaha M1	Pole
1	CATALUNYA GP	Barcelona	46	Gauloises Yamaha Team	Yamaha M1	F.Lap
1	DUTCH TT	Assen	46	Gauloises Yamaha Team	Yamaha M1	Pole; F.Lap
3	U. S. GP	Laguna Seca	46	Gauloises Yamaha Team	Yamaha M1	
1	BRITISH GP	Donington	46	Gauloises Yamaha Team	Yamaha M1	Pole; F.Lap
1	GERMAN GP	Sachsenring	46	Gauloises Yamaha Team	Yamaha M1	race shortened - 25 laps
1	CZECH GP	Brno	46	Gauloises Yamaha Team	Yamaha M1	F.Lap
ret	JAPANESE GP	Motegi	46	Gauloises Yamaha Team	Yamaha M1	
2	MALAYSIAN GP	Sepang	46	Gauloises Yamaha Team	Yamaha M1	
1	QATAR GP	Losail Circuit	46	Gauloises Yamaha Team	Yamaha M1	
1	AUSTRALIAN GP	Phillip Island	46	Gauloises Yamaha Team	Yamaha M1	
2	TURKISH GP	Istanbul Park	46	Gauloises Yamaha Team	Yamaha M1	
3	VALENCIA GP	Valencia	46	Gauloises Yamaha Team	Yamaha M1	

2006

MotoGP: Championship position: 2nd, Wins: 5, Poles: 5, Fastest laps: 4, Points: 220

14	SPANISH GP	Jerez	46	Camel Yamaha Team	Yamaha M1	off on lap 1 - rejoined
1	QATAR GP	Losail Circuit	46	Camel Yamaha Team	Yamaha M1	F.Lap
4	TURKISH GP	Istanbul Circuit	46	Camel Yamaha Team	Yamaha M1	
ret	CHINESE GP	Shanghai	46	Camel Yamaha Team	Yamaha M1	front tyre failure
ret	FRENCH GP	Le Mans	46	Camel Yamaha Team	Yamaha M1	electronics failure; F.Lap
1	ITALIAN GP	Mugello	46	Camel Yamaha Team	Yamaha M1	
1	CATALAN GP	Barcelona	46	Camel Yamaha Team	Yamaha M1	Pole
8	DUTCH TT	Assen	46	Camel Yamaha Team	Yamaha M1	ran off - rejoined lap 3
2	BRITISH GP	Donington	46	Camel Yamaha Team	Yamaha M1	
1	GERMAN GP	Sachsenring	46	Camel Yamaha Team	Yamaha M1	
ret	U. S. GP	Laguna Seca	46	Camel Yamaha Team	Yamaha M1	engine
2	CZECH GP	Brno	46	Camel Yamaha Team	Yamaha M1	Pole
1	MALAYSIAN GP	Sepang	46	Camel Yamaha Team	Yamaha M1	Pole
3	AUSTRALIAN GP	Phillip Island	46	Camel Yamaha Team	Yamaha M1	F.Lap
2	JAPANESE GP	Motegi	46	Camel Yamaha Team	Yamaha M1	F.Lap
2	PORTUGUESE GP	Estoril	46	Camel Yamaha Team	Yamaha M1	Pole
13	VALENCIA GP	Valencia	46	Camel Yamaha Team	Yamaha M1	off on lap 5 - rejoined; Pole

2007

MotoGP: Championship position: 3rd, Wins: 4, Poles: 4, Fastest laps: 3, Points: 241

2	QATAR GP	Losail Circuit	46	Fiat Yamaha Team	Yamaha M1	Pole
1	SPANISH GP	Jerez	46	Fiat Yamaha Team	Yamaha M1	F.Lap
10	TURKISH GP	Istanbul Circuit	46	Fiat Yamaha Team	Yamaha M1	tyre problems; Pole
2	CHINESE GP	Shanghai	46	Fiat Yamaha Team	Yamaha M1	Pole
6	FRENCH GP	Le Mans	46	Fiat Yamaha Team	Yamaha M1	
1	ITALIAN GP	Mugello	46	Fiat Yamaha Team	Yamaha M1	
2	CATALUNYA GP	Barcelona	46	Fiat Yamaha Team	Yamaha M1	Pole
4	BRITISH GP	Donington	46	Fiat Yamaha Team	Yamaha M1	
1	DUTCH TT	Assen	46	Fiat Yamaha Team	Yamaha M1	F.Lap
ret	GERMAN GP	Sachsenring	46	Fiat Yamaha Team	Yamaha M1	crashed out - lap 5
4	U. S. GP	Laguna Seca	46	Fiat Yamaha Team	Yamaha M1	
7	CZECH GP	Brno	46	Fiat Yamaha Team	Yamaha M1	tyre problems
ret	SAN MARINO GP	Misano	46	Fiat Yamaha Team	Yamaha M1	engine
1	PORTUGUESE GP	Estoril	46	Fiat Yamaha Team	Yamaha M1	
13	JAPANESE GP	Motegi	46	Fiat Yamaha Team	Yamaha M1	two pit stops
3	AUSTRALIAN GP	Phillip Island	46	Fiat Yamaha Team	Yamaha M1	F.Lap
5	MALAYSIAN GP	Sepang	46	Fiat Yamaha Team	Yamaha M1	
ret	VALENCIA GP	Valencia	46	Fiat Yamaha Team	Yamaha M1	

2008

MotoGP: CHAMPION, Wins: 9, Poles: 1, Fastest laps: 5, Points: 373

5	QATAR GP	Losail Circuit	46	Fiat Yamaha Team	Yamaha M1	
2	SPANISH GP	Jerez	46	Fiat Yamaha Team	Yamaha M1	
3	PORTUGUESE GP	Estoril	46	Fiat Yamaha Team	Yamaha M1	
1	CHINESE GP	Shanghai	46	Fiat Yamaha Team	Yamaha M1	F.Lap
1	FRENCH GP	Le Mans	46	Fiat Yamaha Team	Yamaha M1	F.Lap
1	ITALIAN GP	Mugello	46	Fiat Yamaha Team	Yamaha M1	
2	CATALUNYA GP	Barcelona	46	Fiat Yamaha Team	Yamaha M1	
2	BRITISH GP	Donington	46	Fiat Yamaha Team	Yamaha M1	
11	DUTCH TT	Assen	46	Fiat Yamaha Team	Yamaha M1	crashed and remounted
2	GERMAN GP	Sachsenring	46	Fiat Yamaha Team	Yamaha M1	
1	U. S. GP	Laguna Seca	46	Fiat Yamaha Team	Yamaha M1	
1	CZECH GP	Brno	46	Fiat Yamaha Team	Yamaha M1	
1	SAN MARINO GP	Misano	46	Fiat Yamaha Team	Yamaha M1	F.Lap
1	INDIANAPOLIS GP	Indianapolis	46	Fiat Yamaha Team	Yamaha M1	Pole; F.Lap
1	JAPANESE GP	Motegi	46	Fiat Yamaha Team	Yamaha M1	
2	AUSTRALIAN GP	Phillip Island	46	Fiat Yamaha Team	Yamaha M1	
1	MALAYSIAN GP	Sepang	46	Fiat Yamaha Team	Yamaha M1	F.Lap
3	VALENCIA GP	Valencia	46	Fiat Yamaha Team	Yamaha M1	

2009

MotoGP: Wins: 1, Poles: 0, Fastest laps: 0, Points: 65

2	QATAR GP	Losail Circuit	46	Fiat Yamaha Team	Yamaha M1
2	JAPANESE GP	Motegi	46	Fiat Yamaha Team	Yamaha M1
1	SPANISH GP	Jerez	46	Fiat Yamaha Team	Yamaha M1

Grand Prix starts: 213, Wins: 98, Pole Positions: 47, Fastest laps: 81, Points: 3438, Average points per race: 16.14
All statistics up to and including SPANISH GRAND PRIX 3/05/2009